Worms & Wormeries

Composting Your Kitchen Waste.........
and more!

By Mike Woolnough

Published by The Good Life Press Ltd. 2010

ISBN 978 1 904871705
A catalogue record for this book is available from
the British Library.

Published by
The Good Life Press Ltd.
The Old Pigsties
Clifton Fields
Lytham Road
Preston
PR4 0XG

www.goodlifepress.co.uk
www.homefarmer.co.uk

Set by The Good Life Press Ltd.
Cover designed by Rachel Gledhill
Printed and bound in Great Britain
by Cromwell Press Group

Contents

Introduction

I wonder how many of you have ventured into your garden on a warm wet night and upon shining a torch around, have been surprised to see worms all over your lawn. On closer inspection, you found that they were stretched out from their hole, over to that of their neighbour, who had also emerged and stretched to meet them, and that the top inch or so of each worm overlapped the other. Did you realise that you had caught the worms in flagrante delicto, or having sex? You were mean enough to stamp your feet and see them instantly zoom back down their burrows, weren't you – a very clear case of coitus interruptus!

Just like the postman knocking on your door early in the morning, you had spoiled the worms' fun. I'm sure that if you had crept out again half an hour later your lawn would have again been the focus of a worm orgy on a Bacchanalian scale.

Interesting as they are, these earthworms aren't the ones that this book is about. They are lobworms, great long fat things that live in permanent deep burrows, going down into the ground many feet. They don't like having these burrows disturbed by spade or rotavator, and so they tend to set up home in soil that is rarely turned over – like your lawn.

They actually do a wonderful job of keeping your soil in great condition. Their holes aerate the soil, and when there is rain the moisture penetrates so much deeper into the soil as it seeps down these tunnels. On top of this the worms help to establish humus in the soil as they come up to the surface and drag tasty goodies like fallen leaves and debris down into their holes. Humus is the broken down organic matter in the top few inches of your soil which is essential for moisture retention and provides nutrients for the plants that you want to grow.

No, these deep-living worms aren't the ones that we want for composting our household and garden waste – they would keep banging their little heads on the bottom of the compost bin wouldn't they?

The worms that we are interested in are those lovely bright red ones that you find when you are out walking in cow fields. You know the ones that I mean, you see them when you flip over a nice hard cowpat with the toe of your boot, and the worms are living happily under their dinner. These beauties are called brandlings, and they are absolutely ideal for composting your waste.

Why should you bother composting your waste?

Well, let me ask you some questions:

Are you concerned about the health of our planet, and would you like to see less waste going into landfill sites?

Are you or somebody in your family, or your neighbours, keen gardeners? If they are fruit or vegetable growers so much the better, but even somebody growing flowers in pots on their balcony will fit the bill.

Are you, or anybody you know, a keen freshwater fisherman?

Do you keep horses or other livestock, and have an ever-increasing heap of manure that you need to get rid of?

If you can answer "yes" to any one of the questions above, then you should be running a wormery and composting your household waste. It's as simple as that.

Foreword

You will have realised, after reading the introduction, that this is not likely to be a boring book, filled with scientific names and dry dusty terms. There is a good reason for this – I don't know them! There might be the odd occasion when I use the Latin name for a creature, but you can rest assured that I will have had to look it up before using it.

The purists may call it vermiculture, but to me it's worms and wormeries.

No, this book will have been written in the way that I approach life: head on, no frills and down to earth – and down to earth is a good place to start when talking about worms.

Worms, you would assume, are a pretty boring theme for a book, and there have been a few raised eyebrows amongst friends when I told them about my latest project.

Perhaps a little background detail would help you to understand where I am coming from.....

I have been living the "Good Life" for the last five or six years, growing my own fruit and vegetables, keeping chickens for eggs and meat, and even venturing into goat keeping for milk and a change of meat diet. All this has been accomplished on four council allotments just down the road from our house, and came about initially because we were disgusted at the way that our food is produced these days. Epidemics of diseases such as foot and mouth and swine fever have led to huge needless wastes of life, and mad cow disease was brought upon us by the feeding of meat products to herbivorous animals! Indeed, the factory farming methods and closure of so many small local abattoirs may have been largely responsible for the spread of these diseases, as animals now have to be transported huge distances to be slaughtered, and the vehicles carrying them to slaughter come into contact with others, sometimes from hundreds of miles away.

Like many other people (indeed, there is a growing army of us) we are happy to eat our own food that has been ethically produced, and shun supermarket food wherever possible.

This self-sufficient lifestyle inevitably led us into other issues such as the greenhouse effect, greener living, food miles and landfill.

The current Labour government (current as I write these notes but likely to be the opposition in the very near future) has chosen to lead the world on green issues, something that it perhaps regrets as it strives to achieve this aim whilst riding out the biggest economic slump in recent years. They have vowed to ensure that a large chunk of our electricity is produced from renewable sources, i.e. wind power, solar power etc., within a few years. They are also turning their attention on the need to reduce waste that goes into our landfill sites, and as well as bringing recycling into the forefront they are looking into charging households for their waste. Many new bins are fitted with technology that can measure the amount of waste contained within. It seems inevitable that, given the financial climate, "pay as you dump" will be with us some time in the near future. Local councils are to be fined for exceeding their landfill quota. Where will those fines be paid from? The money that they receive from Council Tax, of course – in other words from you and I.

This in itself should be a big enough incentive for householders to strive to reduce their waste, but there are even better reasons. A lot of the rubbish that goes into both your rubbish bin and many recycling bins can be turned into a good, useable product that is likely to be of benefit to you or somebody you know – worm cast. Worm cast is the polite name for worm droppings, but before you say "yuk" and throw this book in the bin (the paper recycling bin of course), just consider this fact; this worm poo is just about the most potent fertiliser you could imagine, so potent that it has to be diluted before use. Mixed with other composts such as well-rotted leaf mould it provides a superb growing medium in which plants thrive. Finally, if produced correctly, it is free from weed seeds and is sterile, something that is important if you are trying to grow vegetables in a weed-infested environment. It is so useful that some people will actually pay for sacks of the stuff! Imagine that, turning your rubbish (something that you may soon have to pay to have removed) into a product that may actually earn you some cash and you will have earned a few brownie points too by keeping some waste out of a landfill site.

In reality you are more likely to want to make use of the worm cast yourself, unless you live on the ninety ninth floor of a tower block, but even then you have no excuse as many people grow vegetables in containers on their balconies up in the clouds.

From my own point of view worm cast has another important property. As I said earlier, I grow all my own produce on some council allotments. When I first took them on they were a weed-choked jungle. Leave them a couple of months and they very quickly return to that state as the soil is chock-a-block full of millions of weed seeds that need no second invitation

Worms and Wormeries

to burst forth upon the world. Any disturbance of the soil brings a fresh batch of seeds up to the surface, which then rapidly germinate to produce a fresh batch of weeds. And when I say rapidly I mean just that – they will grow much faster than pretty much any vegetable seed that I am likely to sow into this contaminated soil, quickly choking my crop.

However, if I sow my seeds into a sterile worm cast compost mix, it acts as a mulch, allowing my chosen seed to grow, whilst inhibiting the underlying weed seeds.

To prove this I carried out an experiment. All the weeds from my allotment are composted in conventional compost heaps, but I can never get the mix hot enough to kill off the weed seeds, and so when I use the finished compost all I do is spread weed seeds everywhere.

Stage 1

In preparation for the test I thoroughly hoed a large patch on one of my plots, clearing all existing weeds. I then barrowed in a couple of loads of compost from one of my heaps , dropping it as carefully as possible into a rectangular shape, and marked this out with canes at the corners.

I then carefully laid another rectangle of worm cast at the centre, on top of the compost, and again marked it with canes. As you can see, it is a superb dark colour, full of goodness.

After a couple of weeks or so, you can see the results. Look first at the surrounding area, and you can see that the background weed level is quite high, where the hoeing has disturbed the surface and fresh seeds have emerged and grown. Perennial weeds that were hoed have shot up again and show strong growth. Within the composted area there is a mass of fresh weed growth, far denser than the background levels. However, within the dark worm cast area there is very little weed growth at all, and most of it is either perennials pushing their way through, or in areas where the worm cast was spread a bit thinly.

Stage 2

Stage 3

These results, combined with the superb fertiliser qualities of worm cast, are enough to keep me enthusiastically running several wormeries, both at home and on my allotments, as I can never get enough of the finished product.

Realistically I will never be able to produce enough wormery compost to cover my plots completely, but there are clever ways to use it that make life much easier, which I shall come to later.

Where do I start?

Okay, so I have convinced you that you should be at least composting your kitchen waste, so where do you begin?

I think that the simple answer is to start off with a commercial wormery kit, a pack that comes complete with everything that you will need to get you started. The early part of this book will be dealing purely with ready-made wormeries. The very basic ones consist of little more than a bucket with a sealable lid and a drainage tap near the base.

The more sophisticated types have a series of trays that you gradually add to the system as it gets up and working. The base tray, usually on legs to get it up off the ground so that the tap can be used, is the sump which collects the liquid that drains through - more about this liquid later.

The next tray has a mesh bottom and sits on top of the sump. When first set up this tray contains the bedding layer, usually coconut coir or something similar, which the worms are happy to settle into and chomp their way through. Kitchen waste is then spread on top of the bedding, and an organic mat of some kind is sometimes added on top to retain moisture – the worms usually end up eating that too, very quickly!

I am not totally happy with the use of coir as bedding. It is not what the worms are used to living in, and they may well try to abandon ship very quickly in search of somewhere nicer to live. Coir-based peat substitutes are now growing in use, and the claims are that it is environmentally good to use as it is, after all, a by-product of the coconut industry. The fact remains, however, that it is shipped half way round the world, which cannot be environmentally beneficial.

I have found at least one retailer who supplies their worms in partially composted waste as bedding. The worms and bedding are tipped straight into the wormery with no further bedding required. To me this seems a much better idea as the worms will be comfortable right from the start as their environment will feel familiar, and it will not have contributed to greenhouse gases by being transported thousands of miles.

Usually there is another tray or two that can be added as needed, again with a mesh bottom. The idea is that when the worms have eaten pretty much everything in the base tray, you add a new tray with more food in it and they move up through the mesh base to get to the fresh food. By the time you add the third tray the first one contains finished compost and very few worms. This saves you having to tip the compost out and pick out all the worms, which you have to do with all the simpler systems.

The more thoughtful systems have a ramp of some sort moulded into the sump tray, so that any worms that drop through the mesh of the bottom tray can climb back up rather than drown in the liquid in the sump. Even if they don't make it back to the tray above, they are at least safe on the ramp until you can rescue them. If there is no escape method moulded into your sump shape, place a brick or some cobble stones in the sump and the worms will climb onto them for safety.

If your chosen set-up has holes in the top of the lid and is sited outside you get a lot more liquid in the sump as rainfall slowly flushes through the trays. In a sealed system with side vents the liquid is pure worm juice, highly concentrated. You should always drain the sump at least once a week, and always immediately after any rainfall if your wormery is not waterproof. Even so there are always a few casualties floating around.

Most complete kits will also come with a supply of worm food to help them get started and to provide a treat every couple of weeks, plus they often also include a pack of lime to add from time to time.

It is claimed that adding lime helps to neutralise any acidity building up and keeps your worms happy – you want your worms to be breeding and increasing in numbers all the time, and unhappy worms are less likely to go looking for a mate. However, this is rather misleading as it isn't the acidity that causes problems, so much as the conditions in the wormery that cause the acidity. A lack of oxygen in the bedding is what causes these adverse conditions, and we shall take a look at this in a while.

Wormeries have come a long way in a comparatively short space of time, and their design is constantly improving, with ineffective set-ups being dropped. Most ready-made wormeries should do a reasonable job for you as long as you follow the instructions carefully. Remember that you are looking after live creatures here – you should see them as livestock or pets, and look after them accordingly. You are about to become a farmer – a worm farmer!

The Make-up & Lifestyle
of a worm

Ready to hit the town....

This heading conjured up a mental image for me of worms putting on their powder and lipstick, shimmying into a miniskirt and boob tube and dancing the night away, and has completely ruined my concentration......

There are more than thirty types of worm native to the UK – hard to believe, isn't it? A lot of them will do a job for you in your wormery, but they will not really be in their element and thrive. The worms that interest us are those varieties that will quickly set up a breeding colony and devour our waste products. I use the term "quickly" a little tongue in cheek, as everything is relative and a wormery is not a speedy system. What I mean is that we want worm species that will thrive in the confines of our wormery and enjoy the waste that we feed them, so much so that they will breed plentifully, and eat ever more waste.

So how does a worm eat our waste? Well the answer is that actually it doesn't really, which may surprise you. The worms actually mostly eat the microbes, bacteria and fungi that thrive on the surface of rotting material, together with small amounts of the food itself that have rotted. A worm isn't capable of sitting down to a lunch of fresh vegetables - they have to have it rotted down to a gooey mess first! Some of the micro-organisms that are eaten by the worms remain alive as they pass through the worms' gut, further breaking down the organic material, and are ejected via the anus. Others are digested before being passed as faeces, or worm cast, where more organisms take over again. It is a constantly ongoing and changing chemical mix. The more varied the content of your bin, the bigger the range of microscopic life that will be feeding on it and breaking it down, living and dying, and the larger the menu for your worms. The worms are actually effectively moving around in a soup of micro-organisms, much of which is food to them. The important thing is that they should be aerobic bacteria, organisms that require oxygen to survive. If the conditions in your wormery become hostile and low in oxygen, then anaerobic bacteria will move in and things will very quickly deteriorate, to the detriment of your worm population. Wet conditions in the wormery will very quickly lead to anaerobic bacteria setting up home.

More worms are lost because of anaerobic conditions than any other problem that can affect your wormery.

The waste in your worm bin needs to be damp but not waterlogged, with plenty of tiny air pockets throughout the mix. Kitchen waste contains a high proportion of water which will fill and clog these air spaces, so other materials have to be added to keep the balance just right. I'll deal with this in depth when we come to the feeding section.

When you put your fresh vegetable trimmings, fruit and other bits and pieces into the wormery, the worms can't eat them immediately. Their mouth and digestion can't cope with it until half a million microbes have done their job and the food is decomposing, then you will see the worms in amongst the top layer looking for succulent titbits.

A worm is basically one long digestive tract, with no less than five hearts and a couple of bits of sexual organs along the way.

"A couple of bits?" I hear you asking. Well yes, because worms are actually bi-sexual, having the reproductive organs of both genders. Okay, if you really want to get technical that means that they are hermaphrodites, but this is a book about worms, not the birds and the bees.

Worms and Wormeries

When you saw those worms on the surface that I mentioned in the introduction, they were both passing over sperm to their partner.

Talk about having your cake and eating it too! I guess I'd better draw a diagram or two to explain what I mean......

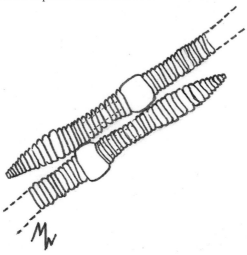

The worms stretch out with their heads overlapping one another. They may be just head to head as above, or they might literally be nose to tail, depending on the species. In some types the sex organs roughly line up, but in most they don't. They both then secrete mucous from the clitellum (the swollen "collar") which helps to keep them firmly fixed together. Mating between worms can take up to three hours. This is because the sperm sometimes has to travel some distance before reaching its destination, which surprisingly is not the female sex organs. The sperm travels from the spermathecal openings in the donor worm until it reaches the sperm sacs of the receptor, where it is stored until the worm is ready to breed. What follows then is truly amazing. The clitellum produces a mucous layer around itself, which gradually hardens, and it fills this layer with albumen. When it is ready, the worm backs out of this hardening layer, and as the ring passes down its body both sperm and eggs are deposited inside. As the ring passes over the worm's head both ends are sealed and it becomes a cocoon containing up to twenty eggs, which are fertilised inside the cocoon. The cocoon is yellow and lemon-shaped and does, in fact, look like a tiny lemon, about an eighth of an inch long. The colouring gradually darkens, and then the worms hatch, usually only one or two from each cocoon, although there may have been more eggs inside. Incidentally, don't expect to see this mating happening on the surface of your worm bin – whilst the huge lobworms in your garden mate on the surface, this

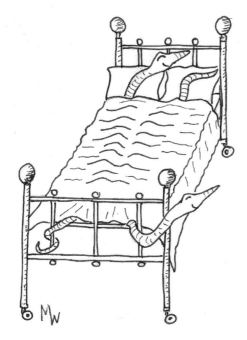

is because of their solitary lifestyle in deep burrows. The redworms in your wormery will mate in the bedding layer - well mating in bed is more natural, isn't it?

The time between laying and hatching varies from species to species, and also according to conditions, but when I tell you that young worms are sexually mature in three to six weeks, and that the population of your wormery can double in three months in ideal conditions, you can see that the whole process is quite fast. If the wormery is kept in the worms' temperature "comfort zone" of around 20 degrees centigrade, and all other wormery conditions are satisfactory, then worms will breed all the year round, munching their way through your waste non-stop. Of course, conditions in the wild in the UK are not ideal as we get cold wet winters and periods of hot dry weather – this is where the cocoon reproduction system comes into its own as the cocoons can withstand these severe conditions and hatch out when a more favourable climate prevails. During drought or freezing temperatures the adult worms dive deep to seek safety, or head for the nice damp warm conditions in the bottom of manure and compost heaps.

In fact, manure heaps are perfect places to look for the sort of worms that we want in our wormeries. We need species that feed on a rich banquet, rather than the types that can exist on a few crumbs. We want them to power their way through our kitchen waste, not take months and months to eat each tray of goodies.

If you start off with a wormery kit, which I strongly advise, then this will also include a pack of worms – usually containing around 1000 composting worms of varying ages. These worms should arrive in prime condition, with a fair proportion ready to start breeding and multiplying. Once you have built up your stock of worms you can perhaps experiment with some of the home made wormeries that I will tell you about later,

Worms and Wormeries

using some of your ever-increasing supply of worms to start them off.

If you are not in a hurry and you fancy starting off your own small system to begin with instead of buying a kit, then of course you can do so. I don't know how they find it, but if a manure heap is built somewhere new the worms for miles around seem to be able to home in on it! I have built fresh heaps of goat muck, and when I started using it on my vegetable plots some months later I found it was full of lovely red brandling worms and yellow-tailed dendrobes. If you know a farmer or somebody who keeps horses, then an hour spent digging in the oldest parts of their muck heaps would provide you with plenty of worms to get you started. Take a bit of the muckheap too to give them starter bedding that they are used to. You will understand why this is important later.

To be honest though, the worm packs available from wormery retailers are so reasonably priced that you would do best to just buy your worms from them, and know that you are getting exactly the right type of worms to make the best use of your kitchen waste.

The main species used in wormery kits in the UK are:

Eisenia fetida, or Brandling. Their colour varies from pink through to almost purple, but it is the yellowish stripes that give it its other name – Tiger Worm. If this worm is attacked it exudes a smelly liquid through its skin that is aimed at deterring predators. This smelly or foetid liquid gives this worm its Latin name. This species is the king of the wormery as it fits the bill for what we need – a greedy eater that breeds rapidly and thrives in our climate.

Eisenia andrei, or Red Tiger Worm. Identical to the above species in all respects, except that it doesn't have the yellow stripes.

Dendrodrilus rubidus is another British worm included in kit packs, commonly referred to as "Dendrodes". They are pink to red in colour, with a yellow tail tip. They are suitable composters as they are often found in manure heaps and other rich food sources, although they are not such prolific breeders as the above two varieties. In a mixed wormery this would matter very little, and they would probably be beneficial as they would eat slightly different foods to the others, ensuring that everything in your waste bin gets composted. The more variety in your bin the better, and the greater the nutrient value will be of your finished compost.

Most worm suppliers will sell a mix of these three types, but make sure that you are not buying from a supplier of fishing bait as they are likely to be selling a different variety. Fishermen love the huge lobworms that live in your lawns and engage in midnight orgies, and these are unsuitable for your wormery. If in doubt ask your supplier for the Latin classification for his worms, as common names vary greatly around the country.

Whilst other native UK species might do okay in your wormery, they are unlikely to prosper in the way that the above three species will, and as I've said before, what we want are happy worms.

One other species that is sometimes used in UK bins is Eisenia hortensis or European Nightcrawler (not to be confused with the North American Nightcrawler or the African Nightcrawler) as it is a favourite bait with fishermen. However, this species prefers very moist conditions and so will always migrate to the bottom of the trays where it will often drop into the sump and drown, or at the very least be difficult to work with as it won't move up through the trays in the obliging manner of the other species, and you will be forced to tip your finished compost out and pick the worms from it. If you are an angler and would like to try your hand at breeding nightcrawlers you would probably do best to use a simple single bin system as described later, where you will be better able to maintain the conditions that these worms prefer.

So, you know which species of worms to start with, and you know how they reproduce – what else do you need to know? Well, it's not really a case of needing to know as such, but worms are actually quite complex creatures, and not at all boring.

For instance, how do they move through the earth? Do they eat their way through? Swim? In fact it is neither – they pull themselves through. You may think that a worm is smooth and slippery, which indeed it is as it coats itself with a layer of mucous, but in fact each tiny segment of the worm has tiny bristles protruding from it known as setae. These bristles are central to their movement. At the front or mouth end of a worm is a very tough "point" that they can force between the particles of earth. The bristles on the first segment then come into play and can be braced against the soil. The whole body then begins a series of muscular contractions and pulls itself in, with each successive set of bristles joining in as it makes contact. By contracting and relaxing alternate setae the worm can make surprisingly fast progress. Unlikely as it sounds, if you lay a worm on a sheet of paper and listen carefully, you may hear the scratching sound that these hairs produce. Offer to demonstrate it to a friend on April the first and they will be convinced that you are playing an April Fool's Day trick – whoever heard of worms scratching?

Worms and Wormeries

The worm is aided by a layer of mucous which is secreted through the skin along the whole of its length. This mucous serves several purposes; it lubricates the worm, helping it to slide through the soil; it adheres to the sides of the wormhole, binding the soil particles together and setting to form a tunnel; and it helps to retain moisture within the worm.

This last point is most important as worms' bodies are mostly made up of water – up to 80% or more when fully moist – but they are very poor at retaining it. A lot is lost through the skin and the anus, and they also waste a lot in urine, which passes through special pores in their skin. Worms have to live in moist conditions so that they can keep absorbing fresh water through their skin, as well as through their food. On the other hand most species don't like stagnant waterlogged soil – this is because they breathe through their skin and stagnant water contains very little oxygen.

Worms can in fact live for a short while in water. If one accidentally falls into a bubbling stream for instance, where the water is well aerated through turbulence, the worm will still be able to absorb oxygen through its skin and survive for a short while until it gets washed ashore – unless it gets gobbled up by a greedy perch first! This is why fishermen love a nice tasty worm on their hook, as it will continue to wriggle and look appetising far longer than many other live baits.

In stagnant water with little oxygen, the worm cannot siphon in enough oxygen and quickly drowns – hence casualties in the wormery sump. The liquid in the sump is a very potent brew, full of bacteria and microbes, and there will be very little oxygen in it. The sump will be full of noxious gases produced by the rotting waste in the trays above. All in all it is a very hostile environment, and a worm has to escape pretty quickly if it is to survive.

What Food Can I Give my Worms?

You can add a tremendous amount of your household waste to your wormery and turn it into wonderful compost.

You can add:

- Vegetable and fruit trimmings
- Stale bread, biscuits, cornflakes, flour etc.
- Used tea leaves and teabags
- Empty cardboard toilet roll tubes, cereal boxes, egg cartons.
- Newspapers (shredded)
- Vacuum cleaner dust bag contents
- Human hair clippings
- Lawn clippings in small quantities
- Coffee grounds and filters
- Natural fibre clothing
- Eggshells, baked and crushed
- Fresh manure
- Tree leaves, especially when rotted to form leaf mould
- Farmyard manure, well rotted
- Rabbit, hamster, Guinea pig droppings
- Meal waste – plate scrapings, but not meat or fish
- Home brew waste – boiled hops
- Certain non-acidic home wine-making pulp residue can also be added

You should not add:

- Too much citrus fruit
- Dog or cat faeces
- Meat
- Fish
- Large quantities of lawn clippings
- Glossy magazines, any colour-printer paper
- Salt – be very careful about anything salty, as salt will kill your worms
- Sawdust or wood shavings
- Garden weeds – the seeds will stay active and pollute your compost
- Wood ash
- Milk, yoghourt or butter
- Onions

Worms and Wormeries

Nothing could be more natural than a wormery system that is run correctly. For millions of years the jungles and rain forests that have covered the Earth have thrived despite storms, fires and earthquakes. The trees and undergrowth grow tall, mature and then die and fall. The fruits of the trees and bushes fall to the forest floor and rot, where they are joined by the corpses of animals and birds of all species. The many creatures on the forest floor burrow through and break down the fallen debris, and eventually the actions of microscopic bacteria and worms return the whole lot to the soil in the form of rich dark humus, where the seeds from the plants and trees germinate and start the whole process all over again. The various waste products that we feed to the worms in our wormeries copy this chain of life and decay in a tiny microcosm.

As with most things in life, anything in moderation is good for you, or at least relatively harmless, and so it is with wormeries. Generally speaking you shouldn't add anything in large quantities in one feed. A little of this and a touch of that is the way to go. Add a layer of kitchen waste, then some shredded paper or cardboard, a toilet roll tube or two, a few grass cuttings and so on.

Citrus fruit should only be added to wormeries in very small quantities, if at all, as it will contribute to acidic conditions. Certainly worms don't find it appetising, and will only eat it when all other food sources have run out. I add small quantities of orange peel from time to time, but none of the orange fruit segments. Adding carbon-rich products like newspaper and cardboard helps to keep the wormery in balance, and traps air pockets. Kitchen waste contains a high percentage of water which can make the wormery waterlogged and cause anaerobic bacteria to thrive, which are harmful to worms. Cardboard and paper will absorb much of this water, and then become worm food as they decompose. Some worms can in fact live purely on damp paper and cardboard, but the redworms that we use in our bins require rich food and will thrive and breed faster given all the "goodies" that we add.

Your wormeries should be fed small quantities regularly rather than a great heap of food occasionally when you remember that your worms are starving. We have a small lidded bin sitting outside our back door and all suitable bits and pieces are emptied into it. It fills up in about a week, and it is then time to feed the worms. During that week it will have started to rot down nicely, and so will be worm heaven when it is added to your wormery.

We know that when the bin is full it is just the right time to share the contents out between our garden wormeries.

What Food Can I Give my Worms?

When you first start out with a wormery it is difficult to know when to add food. A newly set up wormery, with coir or similar bedding, requires very little food initially as the worms will be munching their way through the bedding and converting it into the nesting material that they prefer. Just add a little waste on top to begin with.

If you started your wormery off with worms and worm compost taken from an earlier wormery you should start feeding straight away.

After this, a good way to know when you need to add food is to take a look at where the worms are feeding. If you take the lid off your bin and the worms are in amongst the recently added food, then it is okay to add more. If they are down in the lower levels, then don't feed them any more for now.

As I said, kitchen waste is largely water, and this can cause problems. Plastic wormeries inevitably "sweat." and water condenses on the inside of the lid and sides, and then drains downwards. Add to this the fact that some wormeries have ventilation holes in the lid, and in rainy weather you can have a waterlogged wormery very quickly. It is essential to regularly add shredded paper and/or cardboard to the mix. Generally speaking it is best to leave your worms undisturbed as much as possible, but if the system becomes waterlogged you have little option but to dig it up a bit to get air into the contents, and to mix in some fresh shredded paper to absorb the excess moisture.

Worms in your garden obtain the grit that they need to grind food in their gizzard from your soil, but in the wormery you have to provide it artificially. One way you can solve the problem is by adding a handful of fine sand occasionally. The sand sold for use in the bottom of a bird cage is ideal as it contains grit as well. Don't be tempted to use sand from the beach as it will contain lethal levels of salt, and it is actually illegal to remove it anyway. Builder's sand is also unsuitable. You could add a handful of soil from your garden occasionally, but you don't know what other wildlife you may be introducing in the form of eggs or larvae. Personally, I find that powdered baked eggshells will supply enough grit for your system if used regularly.

Your worm kit will almost certainly have come with a pack of worm food or worm treat. This is advertised as a carefully mixed feed in pellet form, which contains vital nutrients to keep your worms in tip-top condition. Personally I don't believe a word of it! Your kitchen waste will provide a rich feast supplying everything that a worm needs to keep it healthy. As far as I am concerned, pellets just help to soak up a bit of moisture, and

Worms and Wormeries

yes, they will be eaten. You may as well use them – sparingly – by adding a few every now and then to the mix in your wormery, but don't bother buying any more.

As I already mentioned, worms thrive in soil that is slightly acid, around pH5 or 6. This is the scale that tells you whether your soil is acidic or alkaline, and pH neutral is smack dab in the middle, number 7 in a scale of 1 (very acid) to 14 (alkaline). Don't get "hung up" on pH levels though, and don't bother getting a testing kit to keep a check on your wormery levels.

A so-called "essential" that you are likely to receive with your wormery is a bag of lime. This will supposedly help to prevent acidic conditions developing inside your worm bin as lime is alkaline. However, we don't really know what it does to the bacteria and mould mix living in your waste, and adding it is sure to have a pretty traumatic effect on your worms, which although used to acclimatising to different pH levels as they travel through the soil, don't like very rapid changes. Suddenly altering the pH may have repercussions that we don't understand.

Leave the lime in the bag and keep the pH level in your wormery stable by being sensible with the waste mix that you add. It is far better to prevent the problem starting in the first place by operating a sensible feeding regime than to try to instantly create a cure.

Unless your wormery is sited somewhere to keep it warm, the metabolism of your worms will gradually slow down as the colder weather moves in, and their feeding rate will also reduce and eventually stop. It is pointless adding more food at this time and will do more harm than good. During the very cold months much of our kitchen waste goes into our traditional garden "dalek" composter.

Please bear in mind that I personally prefer to err on the side of safety, and some other books will advocate adding things to their wormeries that I advise against. So let's take a look at the foods listed in the table above in a little detail......

What Food Can I Give my Worms?

Vegetable and fruit trimmings

Remember that anything alive and viable will not be eaten by the worms. Pips and seeds are the classic example, and they will remain within your finished compost. The things you are less likely to think about are carrot and other root vegetable tops, which will start to grow and send out fresh foliage in your bin. This doesn't matter at all as they will get buried by the next lot of food that is tipped in and eventually rot down. Similarly, potato peelings that have "eyes" will germinate. Ours don't make it into our bins as they are cooked to be fed to the chickens. It's a good idea to cook them before adding to your worm bin too. Don't add the leaves from potatoes, tomatoes or rhubarb to your worm bins as they are poisonous, and be very careful with leaves from exotic shrubs in your garden as they may be similarly toxic.

Pretty much any kitchen trimmings are okay to use, but avoid too much citrus fruit as already mentioned. Onions are a debatable subject. The outer skin is fine to use in compost, but avoid adding too much inner flesh. As with citrus peel, the worms will avoid it until it has been well broken down by other organisms, and it can add an unwanted unpleasant smell to your wormery.

Stale bread and bakery products

Your worms will love you for feeding them with this! Chop it into smaller pieces to increase the surface area for moulds and bacteria to work on it and break it down. Be careful that you don't include anything salty as salt will kill your worms.

Tea leaves and teabags

These are another worm favourite. Tear the bags open, but don't tip the leaves out. Use the whole bag as it is another source of carbon and the worms love to curl up inside.

Cardboard

Toilet rolls, egg cartons, cereal boxes etc. are all fine to use in small quantities throughout the layers in your bin. Corrugated cardboard is good too as the worms will use the holes in between the layers as tunnels.

Be careful not to add too much at a time as it will bind together and form a solid lump. It is a good idea to cut cardboard into one inch wide "sticks" before adding it to your wormery as this will create more air spaces.

Newspapers

Newspaper and cardboard is an essential ingredient for your wormery, especially if you are not adding anything else that is "woody." Newspaper should not be added whole, or as with cardboard the layers will stick together and form a mass that won't break down very quickly. Newspaper (and thin card) should be shredded and "fluffed up" before adding to the wormery to ensure that there are lots of lovely air pockets. Don't use the glossy magazine inserts, or in fact any colour magazines as the inks may be toxic to worms. Whilst most printing companies are changing over to non-toxic inks I believe it's better to be safe than sorry. The coloured pages in newspapers are fine to use.

The best method for adding shredded newspaper is to dampen it and lay it on top of the fresh kitchen waste, as it will then act as a moisture mat. The next time that you top up the bin with food waste, simply spread it on top of the paper and then add a new top layer of paper.

Some wormeries are supplied with a moisture mat, but the worms will soon eat it and the shredded paper will take its place nicely.

Vacuum cleaner contents

Lots of lovely hair, dust, crumbs and skin particles, and probably dirt and grit too. Lovely stuff to add in, but of course be sensible and don't add it if you have just used the vacuum to clear up a load of spilled washing powder or anything else toxic!

Human hair clippings

My wife cuts my hair, and the clippings go straight into the worm bins.

I see no reason why animal hair shouldn't go in too. Certainly chicken breast feathers often find their way into my bins in small quantities, especially during the annual moult when their feathers are everywhere.

The obvious usual warnings apply regarding any potentially harmful shampoos or treatments that have been used prior to clipping. It might sound gross, but nail clippings can go in too – they are only modified hair, after all.

Lawn clippings

These are a controversial subject. A light sprinkling of clippings in between other layers of waste is perfectly acceptable. Tip the entire contents of your lawn mower clippings box into your wormery and you will almost certainly kill the whole population. Why? Well, grass clippings heat up dramatically for a while during the initial decomposition – try adding a load to the top of your traditional compost heap and plunge your hand in a few days later and the heat will amaze you. If you compost your clippings conventionally until they have dried and shrivelled up, they can then be safely added to your worm bin, but as always – in moderation.

Coffee grounds and filters......lovely stuff, espresso worm food.

Clothing

Anything wool, cotton or linen will retain moisture and be decomposed and digested, but will take some time. Clothing recycling bins or charity shops would probably be a more ethical way of disposing of your unwanted Prada and Gucci. Don't forget that buttons, zips and fasteners will be rejected out by your worms, and any man made fabrics are a definite no no. Go back a couple of hundred years and worn out clothing and leather footwear was always dug into the crop fields to improve the soil – it is why treasure hunters find so many buttons and buckles when using their metal detectors in fields.

Bleep, bleep.....Is it the Hoxne Hoard? No, it's another damned button!

Eggshells

I prefer to bake and crush mine before adding them to the bins..... well actually I put them through the blender to reduce them to a fine dust. They are great for the worms as they provide calcium and the grit that they need to digest their food.

Eggshells will still be present in the finished compost, so I like them to be small particles. Incidentally, this is the only worm food that you should put through the blender. Using a chopper or shredder is good as it increases the surface area for microbes to work on, but a blender will usually only produce a liquid stodge that will clog the air pockets and lead to an invasion of anaerobic bacteria.

Fallen leaves

Small quantities of leaves will be processed and enjoyed, but avoid the tougher oak and beech as they take longer to decompose and contain a lot of tannin. The resin in pine needles is to be avoided as well. Composted leaves, or leaf mould, will be thoroughly enjoyed by your worms. Add them to your traditional compost heap, or compost them separately. A great way is to fill a black bin bag with leaves, give the contents a good watering with a watering can, tie the bag, punch some holes in it with a garden fork, and then stick it in a corner somewhere and forget about it for six months. Your worms will think Christmas has come early when you feed them the resulting compost.

A point worth noting is that you will possibly also be adding alien life forms to your wormery, which might not be so good if your wormery is indoors.

Worms and Wormeries

Manure

I'm going to include all types of faeces under this heading and deal with them individually. Some animal dung contains organisms that are harmful to humans, and some contains high quantities of "hot" ingredients that will kill your worms if used fresh.

Horse manure is wonderful stuff, but you will usually acquire it mixed up with the animal's bedding, which may be sawdust based – see separate heading. It will almost certainly contain a lot of urine. Pile it up in a heap for 3 months and then add a little to your wormery every couple of weeks. Individual "dollops" collected from a field loose only need to be left outside for a month to allow the rain to leach out anything unpleasant before using them.

Goat, pig, sheep, and cow manure can be treated as above, but remember that pig and cow muck is very smelly and may not be suitable if your wormery is sited close to your house.

Rabbits, guinea pigs, hamsters etc. are also vegetarians, and their cage cleanings can be added to the worm bin. Rabbits seem to urinate more than any other domesticated animal and their "toilet corner" is usually sodden when cleaned out. Leave it out in the open to be rained on a few times, after which it will be safe to use.

Chicken muck is probably the "hottest" and strongest of all the animal manures, but it is also wonderful stuff! It needs to have the strong elements leached out of it before use. Again, it is a case of piling it up out in the open air for two or three months to allow the rain to give it a good rinsing. I use freshly fallen leaves as a litter inside my chook houses and on the floor of their runs. Mixed up with uneaten fruit and veg, moulted feathers and the chicken droppings it creates a wonderful mix that the worms just love once it has cooled down.

Dog and cat faeces should never ever be added to a kitchen waste wormery. I will say that again for good measure – do NOT add dog or cat muck to a kitchen waste wormery. Both may contain pathogens that can be extremely harmful to humans, especially children. The whole point of a kitchen waste wormery is to produce compost to feed your vegetables, so it would be madness to introduce harmful organisms into your veg bed. It is quite likely that these nasty bugs are destroyed in a worm's stomach, but nobody yet knows for sure as there has been no detailed research in a laboratory, so why take the risk? We operate a totally separate wormery for our dog's droppings, and the resulting compost is used around the base of fruit trees on our allotments. It should never be spread anywhere that children play, as their less well developed immune system is more susceptible.

Dog and cat faeces may contain the Toxicara roundworm in the form of adults, eggs or larvae. If ingested they can cause a wide range of illnesses including weight loss, asthma, coughing, headache, fever, pain, nausea and, in severe cases, blindness.

If the above has alarmed you, then I am pleased because I cannot stress enough the danger that Toxicara presents. Many cat and dog owners are somewhat lax over worming their pets, so the danger is ever present.

Incidentally, dog and cat poo should not be used when the animal has been recently wormed. The active ingredient in worming tablets which kills intestinal worms will also wipe out your garden worm colony.

Why bother at all with dog and cat poop? Well it depends on your point of view, I suppose. We feel strongly that nothing should go into landfill that could be disposed of elsewhere. Yes, you can bury the poo in your garden, but you will invariably at some point accidentally exhume some whilst digging a fresh hole for the next consignment, and the point about children playing still applies. You could perhaps use a specially designed pet toilet, but at the end of the day, why waste what is a useful asset if it is dealt with properly?

Many people may find the idea distasteful, but this is probably due to the unpleasant smell of dog and cat faeces.

Bird droppings from caged birds, particularly parrots and parakeets, should also not be composted as they may also contain pathogens dangerous to humans, namely Chlamydophila psittaci which causes Psittacosis, better known as parrot fever.

Human dung is another unpleasant subject, but for hundreds of years the contents of night soil chamber pots were spread on our fields.

I know that in some places human faeces are again being composted, but it's not something that I personally fancy doing. I suppose that if you wanted to, the rule of a separate wormery applies. Bearing in mind the vast quantities of artificial additives and preservatives that most people consume in their food these days, I can't help wondering whether worms would really find our waste products palatable, or whether the finished compost would be any safer to use than dog poo compost.

Meal waste

Plate scrapings and uneaten cooked food can safely be added to your worm bin. I would avoid anything salty or very spicy, but that is probably me being super-cautious. Very small amounts of meat within the scraps can be ignored.

Home brew residue

Boiled hops from home brewed beer can be added safely to your wormery. The yeast sediment from the bottom of a wine making demijohn will also be eaten with relish by your worms, but, again being super-cautious, I don't use the lees from orange or lemon-based home made wine.

Meat and Fish

I've lumped these two together as in my mind they should be treated the same. Small quantities scraped from dinner plates are safe to feed to your worms. Personally I am paranoid about attracting rats to my worm bins – apart from anything else, if rats get in they will consider your precious worms to be the dessert course! Meat and fish smell strongly as they decompose and, whilst we dislike the smell, to a rat it is the equivalent of somebody ringing the dinner gong. And I haven't yet even mentioned flies and ants......

Every gardening book says do not add meat or fish to a conventional compost heap, so why should a worm composting system be any different? Meat bones take ages to decompose and would still be whole when that particular tray of your composting system is ready for use on the garden. The fact that archaeologists dig up human skeletons thousands of years old proves that bones don't decompose well. Chicken and other poultry bones decompose much faster and so could possibly be used, but I don't advise it. However, fish bones are so tiny that they would probably be okay.

If you really must add meat, then be sure to bury it in the top layer rather than just tipping it in so that it sits on the surface. Alternatively, cover with a layer of soil or compost.

Sawdust, wood shavings and woodchip

I'm going to be controversial here. Some woods contain resin that is quite toxic – can you be sure which types have gone into your mix?

I have read that wood also uses oxygen as it decomposes. Some books advocate using woodchip as a bedding material, and it would certainly create plenty of air spaces that would help with drainage and aeration, but you would have to be prepared to pick through your finished compost to remove the wood before using it. Sawdust can bind together and create anaerobic conditions which we have to avoid at all costs. Shavings fall somewhere between the two so is it really worth the risk?

For me the answer is "no," although I add sawdust from animal bedding to my normal compost heaps, but it takes a long time to break down.

Weeds

Small quantities of weeds that have not flowered or seeded are suitable to add to the normal mix of waste, but generally they don't have much substance to them, and there are far better things to feed to our greedy worms, which require rich foodstuffs. They will, however, add to the humus content of the finished compost, and again are likely to increase the number of air pockets inside the bedding, particularly if of a woody nature. The sensible answer is to use in moderation.

Wood or coal ash

Another item that is subject to debate, with some saying it is acceptable and others not. Personally, I look at it this way; there is a substance called diatomaceous earth which consists of the fossilised remains of tiny creatures called diatoms. It is sold as a remedy for lice and mites in poultry because it contains microscopically sharp particles which pierce the external skeletons of these tiny insects, causing them to dehydrate and die. If anybody can convince me that ashes don't contain the same type of sharp particles, which could kill tiny baby worms, then I would be happy to use them in my wormery, but until then I will spread the ashes from my bonfires around my vegetables to help keep slugs and snails away.

Dairy products

Have you smelled butter, cream or yoghurt that has been out of the fridge for a week? I rest my case. In my mind they constitute the same risk as meat and fish.

Home Sweet Home

So let's take a closer look at some of the ready-made wormeries that are available in the UK. There are three main types of wormery; the throughflow system where the compost is harvested in a continuous cycle from the bottom of the bin, dump and sieve where you have to somehow separate the compost from the worms and the upwardly mobile tray system where trays of food are progressively stacked up. As the contents of each tray are consumed and converted into compost, the worms move up into the one above. The bottom tray is eventually harvested and popped back on the top of the stack and re-filled with kitchen waste.

All of them add food to the top layer. The dump and sieve and tray systems generally have a sump and/or tap so that the worm juice can be drained off and collected, whilst with a throughflow type the juice does just that – flows through and drains away. The dump and sieve method involves tipping the whole wormery contents out and hand picking the worms from the compost, or sieving it with a small-meshed garden riddle. Either way, pretty much all of the cocoons and tiny young worms are going to be lost when the compost is used on the garden. You also face the problem of restarting the whole system again each time you harvest your compost. The best method is to return the top layer of the compost to the bin, as this will obviously be exactly what the worms are used to living in, and will contain a fair amount of partially decomposed waste so that they have a ready-to-eat food supply. If you have left the wormery too long before emptying and all the waste has been fully converted into vermicompost, then you would probably do best to start again with completely fresh bedding, mixing some of the old compost in with it to make the worms feel at home.

Let's take a look at just a few of the many ready-made wormeries that are available. The basic principals will apply to other designs and help you to select the right wormery for you.

Waste Juggler

Basically this is a small wheelie bin rubbish bin that has been adapted into a wormery. Much larger than the under the sink type bins, it can compost quite a large amount of waste. The problem with a tall narrow composter is that there is not much surface area, which restricts the worm population to a certain extent as

oxygen will be limited. It is also much more likely to lead to a waterlogged and/or anaerobic bin. The idea is that you add the supplied drainage chips, place the woven bin liner inside your bin on top of them and then add nesting material, worms and food waste into the bag. The chips create a kind of sump area which can be drained via the tap. To use the compost you have to tip the whole contents out and sort through them to separate the worms from the compost. This particular model seems to have ceased production as I can't find any listed by retailers on the Internet, but you may find one for sale on the secondhand market.

I'm going to include in this section the small "under the sink" units that are marketed under various names and sold as being suitable for one person, flats, children, and such like. In my opinion, and I stress that this is my opinion, they are not really suitable as permanent wormeries. The fact that they are often advertised as sealed so that worms can't get out, and yet only have a small ventilation valve, is a classic recipe for an anaerobic bin. If bought as a first wormery they may well put the buyer off keeping worms for life by producing an atrocious smelly mess full of dead worms. Even if managed really well they hold a remarkably small volume of waste, especially when you consider that the top few inches will be fresh uncomposted material, and so will need to be re-started at regular intervals by tipping them out and sorting through the contents. They simply don't hold enough to be truly useful.

The Children's Wormery

This inexpensive wormery is basically a brightly coloured converted plastic dustbin with holes drilled for aeration.

Worms and Wormeries

There is no tap as the juice drains away through more holes drilled in the base. Although unsophisticated, the kit comes complete with everything that you need to get started, and the kids will just love picking through the finished compost to sort out the worms ready to start the next batch off. This is a great way to get children interested in environmental issues and teach them the responsibility involved in looking after pets. The 21 litre capacity is a good size, and it is certainly a cheap way to get started in vermicomposting.

Can'o'Worms

The Can'o'Worms is probably the biggest selling of the "upwardly mobile" wormery systems, and has been the "flagship" of vermiculture in the UK for several years due to its ingenious design.

This cleverly-named wormery does in fact look rather like a tin can when all the trays are stacked up.

As this model is fairly typical of all the tray systems I will include step by step setting up details here. The bottom section is the sump, with legs and a tap. Notice the central ramp section which serves as a ladder for worms to get back into the main wormery should they happen to fall into the sump.

The first tray is then added on top. The instructions tell you to use part of the cardboard packaging fitted inside the base to stop worms falling through as soon as they are introduced. This is most important when setting up any tray system, and some makers do not tell you to do so. The coir bedding is very loose and soft and will sift through the mesh, and the worms will fall through with it. Several sheets of newspaper can be used instead

of cardboard, or a piece of cotton cloth would probably be even better as it would take much longer to rot and protect the worms for longer. Whichever you use, in my opinion it is advisable to cut a hole in the paper or cardboard just above the ramp so that worms can climb through from the sump. Notice the plastic supports on the inside of the sump – the first tray slides down and sits on these.

The bedding is now added. The coir usually comes in brick format, which you soak in a bucket of water. It absorbs the water, swells up, and breaks apart – you will be amazed by just how much it expands!

Squeeze most of the water out and drop the coir into the wormery tray, and level it off. It will probably pretty much fill the tray to its load level, but will shrink down considerably as it is processed by the worms.

Although coir is perfectly acceptable as a bedding material there are other bedding materials that you can use, and the best of these is natural worm compost from a wormery that is up and running. When purchasing a wormery it is worth asking your supplier if they will send you a small bag of worm compost rather than the coir block. Other suitable bedding is often readily available in many homes – damp shredded paper or cardboard is acceptable if nothing else is available, but leaf mould or compost from your traditional compost heap would be better. Well rotted manure would certainly get your worms off to a flying start.

Notice again the plastic supports for the next tray, which should always be sitting on top of the composting contents of the tray below when it settles onto these slots. As the food becomes exhausted and the tray contents are converted into pure compost, the worms move up through it, squeeze through the mesh of the tray above and start on the food in that tray. In the Can'o'Worms and several similar systems a gap can sometimes develop between the top of the compost and the base of the next tray and if the worms can't get to the next level they will eventually starve. Adding fresh foodstuff in to fill the gap is defeating the object as the worms will stay at that level to eat the new food instead of migrating upwards, so to prevent this problem developing simply make sure that you fill each tray with waste a couple of inches above the tray supports before adding a fresh tray so that as the compost (and the tray above) settle, they will stay in contact. Inspect it regularly and if there is a gap the solution is quite simple – rake the compost to one side so that it forms a mound. Part of it will then be in contact with the next tray, and the worms can move upwards.

Now the worms are added. Leave the lid off so that daylight will drive them down into the bedding – worms hate light. If you have resident blackbirds or thrushes it might be an idea to stand guard for a few minutes so that the birds don't take advantage of this free meal.

Within five minutes all the worms will have disappeared. It is a good indicator of the resilience of worms that there are seldom any dead worms left on the surface after the others have dug down into the bedding.

Most instructions state that there isn't really any need to add food yet as the coir will keep your worms occupied for a while, but I like to get the wormery started straight away, and I have noticed that the worms are often up and in this top layer within a few days, during which time some of the foodstuff will have started to rot. As the

coir is very moist I like to add a sheet or two of newspaper immediately, and then a small selection of various foods and a light sprinkling of worm treat pellets if these have been supplied with the wormery.

If you add food too soon there is a risk that the worms will eat the food rather than the coir bedding if this was used, so that your first tray of compost will contain a fair bit of undigested coir. As some modern commercial compost contains coir in preference to peat, which is quite rightly being phased out of use, I can't really see where this poses a problem. Not that coir should be used in compost......

That's it. Now position your wormery somewhere sheltered, and just leave the worms to get on with it.

A word of warning - In the first few days the worms may well not like their new home as the pH may not be at the level that they are accustomed to. They will almost certainly try to escape, and when you lift the lid you will find loads of the little blighters stuck to the lid and all round the tops of the side. If they had little spades they would probably try to dig an escape tunnel. This is quite normal and they will very quickly settle down. In the Can'o'Worms there is no escape route, but in some other unlidded systems it is wise to take precautions. This is another reason why the first tray should have a layer of cardboard fitted in the base before filling with bedding or all the worms may well be in the sump by day two!

Store your spare trays somewhere until they are needed. Keep gradually adding waste over a period of time until eventually the food level is a couple of inches above the tray supports, and it is time to add another tray.

Regularly check that the air holes drilled in the lid haven't become clogged up or covered with fallen leaves, and if your wormery is out in the open always drain the sump after heavy rain as it fills up remarkably quickly in severe weather.

As the months go by keep adding trays until they are all in use. When the last (top) one is full, it is time to harvest your first tray full of compost – and an exciting time it is too!

Worms and Wormeries

The three stages of compost: waste food and newspaper; partially rotted waste in which some items may be recognisable; completed vermicompost, with just a few organic bits and pieces still visible.

Stage 1

Stage 2

Stage 3

It may look a little disappointing at first, as there will probably be pieces of uncomposted matter in amongst the worm cast, and it may be sprinkled with eggshell if you have added them with your kitchen waste. It doesn't matter at all – just sieve the whole contents through a fairly fine garden riddle into a bucket or other container, then tip the debris left in the sieve back into the top tray of the stack to compost a bit further.

You now have your first wonderful compost to use and the empty tray simply goes back on top of the stack to start the cycle all over again.

If you are expecting that this process will work quickly, please have a re-think. Even if started in early spring so that you take advantage of the warm period of maximum activity, it is still likely to be six months before you harvest your first compost, and if cold weather intervenes it could be longer still. Composting can only proceed at the rate that your worms are feeding and breeding.

The Worm Factory

This followed on from the Can'o'Worms but was in my opinion a backward step.

Now that the new "Worm Café" (see overleaf) has been launched, some UK retailers are phasing this model out, but I list it just in case the reader is offered one secondhand. The trays have lifting hand holes in the sides and the lid is fitted with a couple of inserts designed to block these holes. They don't work very well, and all manner of wildlife can get in, whilst half my worms escaped on the first night through these openings. Slugs and even snails can get in when still young and small, and then grow too big to get out, but worse still the wormery gets infested with fruit flies that swarm all around you when you take the lid off and can come and go freely through these openings – definitely not a wormery to use indoors! This model doesn't have a ramp in the sump either, which is essential even if it isn't always particularly effective, so place a brick in the sump to give your worms a sporting chance to escape.

Worms and Wormeries

The Worm Cafe

This is the latest model rolling off the production lines of this Australian manufacturer, and is undoubtedly the best to date.

This exploded view of the wormery shows quite well how the system fits together. The top tray is full of kitchen waste, the middle one is semi-composted and the bottom one is compost ready for harvesting. This model has a worm ramp, and as you can see here, they do use it

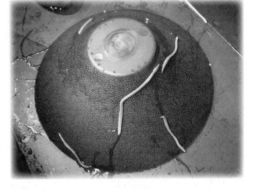

Notice that the large worm in the centre is almost in breeding condition as it has a partially developed clitellum – the bulge just behind the head at the top.

This model has a close-fitting lid and the ventilation holes are in the sides, not the lid.

The Beehive Wormery

Whilst not exactly being ugly, many wormeries aren't really what you would call pretty.

This wormery is definitely the exception as it is attractive enough to use as a feature in your garden. Constructed with a wooden outer casing that conceals internal plastic trays, it closely resembles a standard beehive, and comes in a range of colours. Painted white it would be hard to tell from a real beehive from a distance. The plastic trays slide down inside each other, so the compost is always in contact with the next tray above. There is, however, no lid to the top tray so your worms may possibly escape. This isn't really a problem as you could cut a piece of cardboard to fit and lay it over the top tray, or perhaps be lucky enough to find a biscuit tin lid to fit. In either case, just to be on the safe side, punch some ventilation holes in it to ensure an adequate air supply. The beehive casing has an apex roof so the wormery is well protected from rain. When inspecting the wormery you have to start by dismantling the outer frame first, section by section, to get to the trays, and the sump has no ramp so a brick is needed to help escapee worms to have a rescue island, but overall it is an effective and attractive wormery.

The Worm City Wormery

As wormeries become more and more popular, it is inevitable that fresh models will appear, and this is one of them. Recently designed and manufactured in the UK, it is clear that it is the result of a great deal of thought.

Starting from the bottom, the base is very sturdy – three or four trays of compost can be very heavy, and plastic legs have sometimes been known to buckle. The sump floor has been arranged rather like terraced gardens, which help the worms to escape in easy stages, and the trays slide into one another freely.

The Executive Wormery

This system has nice big tough trays that provide plenty of composting surface area. The sump has no escape ramp, so a brick is needed to avoid the need to give your worms swimming lessons.

This wormery has no legs or base and is designed to sit on

a step or raised platform so that you can use the drainage tap. A nice feature is the snap-lock lid that prevents uninvited visitors of the small two legged or four legged kind.

The Dog Poo Wormery

I can already see some of you wrinkling your noses as you read this paragraph heading. This model is actually the Executive wormery shown, but marketed as a system for composting dog or cat faeces.

The snap-lock lid makes it ideal for this use, as it keeps little fingers away from the contents – the lid is quite stiff to undo – and helps to keep the smells locked inside! It is sold with only one tray, with further trays as an optional extra. Obviously this is designed to keep the initial cost down, but I feel that this is a mistake as in my opinion you should never operate a dog poo wormery with just one tray, and other companies offer similar single tray poo bins. When the contents are composted you would have to use the dump and sort method to retrieve the worms, and this would be very unhygienic. I use this system with at least two trays. In the warm season it can cope with the daily output of my Springer Spaniel, but in the cold of winter we don't use it as the dormant worms would literally be swamped in poo.

We cover the bedding in the first tray with a layer of dog poo, sprinkle soil or leaf mould to cover it, then add shredded paper before starting the next layer. This helps to keep the smell down, and in all honesty I have to say that unwanted aromas haven't been a problem. Dog mess isn't a pleasant thing to deal with, and the contents of the wormery very quickly become unsightly with huge growths of hairy looking mould covering it, but if you have a dog then you are already used to having to deal with their rear-end production line! Wormeries can also be used for cat faeces, but I have no experience of working with one. A cat's mess is smellier than that of dogs, and cats have a habit of wandering off to do their business in other people's gardens, so I'm not convinced that it would work. If you are thinking of filling your wormery with cat faeces removed from a litter tray I would advise you to check the ingredients of the litter filling first to ensure that there is nothing harmful to your worms' good health incorporated in the mix.

Gloves should always be worn when working on a dog poo wormery and the finished compost should only be used in areas where children do not play. Do not use it in your vegetable beds. We use ours around our fruit trees as a top dressing. You should always wash your hands after working on any wormery, but this particularly applies to poo wormeries.

The Waste Buster Wormery

If you fancy running a wormery on a bigger scale, then the Waste Buster is definitely for you.

This wormery is the only commercially-supplied model I know of that works on the "through-flow" system. Manufactured from treated plywood harvested from carefully farmed woodland, the system is not cheap, especially when you look at the larger models, and you should remember that a wooden wormery will need to be re-treated regularly or it will rot.

Having said that, the system holds a lot of waste, and if it works as smoothly as the manufacturers claim, then it should be very easy to run and maintain, and it will never suffer from getting too wet as all liquid drains straight through. Certainly this type of wormery is used quite extensively in America, although I have never tried it.

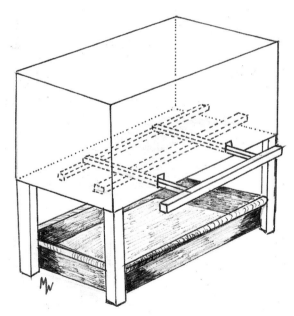

Pushing the harvesting bar backwards and forwards sifts compost through the mesh bottom to land in the tray underneath.

Worms and Wormeries

It is basically a deep wooden box raised on legs with a hinged lid and a mesh floor, with a harvesting bar fitted in the bottom. Once the system has been running for some time you harvest the finished compost by pushing the harvesting bar backwards and forwards, which sieves the compost through the mesh floor into a plastic tray supplied which fits under the wormery. As there is a fitted lid and solid sides, the wormery is unaffected by heavy rain. Any moisture from the decomposing waste drains away through the mesh.

The whole system is well ventilated, and as worms don't like daylight they tend to stay put in the bedding rather than drop out through the mesh floor. I'm very surprised that nobody has produced something similar using recycled plastic as a construction material as this system would then be virtually maintenance-free.

I would be reluctant to place slow-rotting materials into this type of wormery as they may well jam up the harvesting bar in the bottom, which would be difficult to unclog without emptying the whole wormery to remove the offending debris.

Having earlier said that there are three types of system, I am now going to contradict myself slightly and say that there is in fact a fourth way of running a wormery. The "pocket-feeding" system is widely used in America where many worm enthusiasts build their own wormeries. I will cover this method later when I deal with DIY wormeries. Pocket feeding does not really work for the commercial wormeries described above, which are all designed for steady top-feeding, spreading the fresh waste out on top of the older decomposing material.

Visitors - The Good, the Bad, and the Ugly.....

Your wormery will very quickly become a seething maelstrom of life in many of its forms – but if you get fish or mammals in there then you are definitely doing something wrong!

The life that you want present in your wormery consists of the many organisms and creatures that help to break down your kitchen waste and render it edible for your worms. You don't want anything living there that will make the conditions unpleasant for your worms so that they stop eating or, worse still, stop breeding, and you definitely don't want worm predators getting into your wormery.

Before you start panicking I'll quickly tell you that if you are running a purpose-built manufactured wormery, then you will probably never encounter the majority of the creatures I'm going to talk about here. If, on the other hand, you progress to building any of the larger wormeries that I will tell you about later, then you are likely to run into some of them.

We'll start with the smallest inhabitants of your wormery, and these will be present in all wormeries, no matter what type of set-up you have. Don't bother looking for them though, because you will strain your eyes trying to see the majority of them as they are microscopic.

I am, of course, talking about those creatures that I have already mentioned – the microbes. There will be literally millions of them, in fact millions of millions, and we don't even have a scientific name for the vast majority of them.

Your bin will be swarming with bacteria. This doesn't mean that they are going to give you some dreadful illness, although you should of course always wash your hands after working on any of your wormeries. Mention bacteria to most people and they will probably remember that dentists and toothpaste manufacturers are always going on about bacteria and tooth decay. Like a wormery, your mouth is full of millions of bacteria. They are all beavering away, working on the tiny particles of food trapped between your teeth. In themselves they are not harmful, in fact they are beneficial as countless billions of them also live in your gut, breaking down the food that you eat so that your body can absorb the nutrients it needs. This process starts the moment that food enters your mouth, when saliva and bacteria begin their action. The downside is that these bacteria just love sugar, and in the process of eating it they produce lactic acid, which attacks the enamel of your teeth.

In your wormery the vast array of acids and enzymes produced by the huge variety of bacteria is wonderful stuff as it works on the assortment of kitchen waste that you have added, and breaks it down into individual constituents that can feed the ravenous hordes, including your worms. The digested foodstuff that passes through the microbes and is excreted by them is in turn eaten by other microbes and your worms. The bacteria themselves are a rich food source for your worms and myriads of other creatures and of course their excreta also adds to the mix. When conditions deteriorate and anaerobic bacteria start to multiply, the analogy with your teeth returns as they create an acidic environment.

The next stage of wildlife that adds to the mix is the moulds and fungi that are rapidly growing on the kitchen waste. Many of these are visible when you open the lid of your wormery. Those fluffy looking grey or white strands growing everywhere are fungi. Whilst the rest of the floral world was busy developing ways of using sunlight beneficially, the fungi were learning to live in the dark and process their food in other ways. You often see the larger members of the family, ie. mushrooms and toadstools, growing on living or dead trees and stumps – fungi are extremely good at breaking down the cellulose present in wood. Now if you consider that we need to add a lot of paper or cardboard to our wormeries, and paper is made from wood, then you can perhaps see how fungi are extremely useful to us. As we pile more waste into our bins, covering the previous top layer, this fungi itself becomes food for our worms and other organisms.

The mushrooms that we ourselves eat are merely the fruit produced by the organism. The living and growing part is a fine filigree thread that grows underground. When you see a big patch of mushrooms growing in a meadow, they are the fruits of a single fungus spreading itself out underground. They can cover a very large area. Similarly, the fungi in you wormery spread their threads throughout the compost.

Everything becomes "grist to the mill" and nutrition to the other organisms living in your worm bin – most importantly of course, your worms.

Into this soup of activity step the next microbes in size – the protozoa. These tiny single-celled creatures feed upon the teeming millions of bacteria, moulds and fungi. Although still microscopic, the largest of them can reach 1mm in size and so may just be discernible to the naked eye. Certainly, if you bung a little of your compost under a microscope you will see plenty of them moving around, using their whip-like tails for propulsion. Of course our worms find them and hang out the "dinner is served" sign.

If you do take a peek through a microscope at a sample from your bin, you may well spot tiny whirling creatures. They live in the tiny droplets of water present in your bin, and trap their food in the tiny hairs that stick out from their bodies. They are called rotifers, and look like tiny wheels.

If you notice any tiny eel-like creatures in your sample, they will almost certainly be nematodes. Every keen gardener will have heard of nematodes these days as they are the current buzzword amongst those seeking organic pest control methods. The ones you hear about the most are those that prey upon slugs. You buy a sachet of these microscopic parasites, tip them into your filled watering can and then water the whole area where slugs are a pest. The tiny worms move through the soil, searching for young slugs living under the surface. When they find them they literally move in – getting inside the slug via the respiratory tract, where they rapidly start breeding. Within a few days the slug stops feeding and becomes inactive. Not long after this it dies, and as it decomposes a fresh wave of newly born nematodes are born and move out into the soil seeking fresh prey.

But there are hundreds of thousands of nematode species, all living and feeding upon different things. Many types will be living in your worm bin, all making their unique contribution to the food chain and the eventual decomposition of your kitchen waste.

Worms and Wormeries

Very dramatic isn't it?

Coronation Street's twisting and turning plots are child's play compared to the complex interaction of flora and fauna taking place inside your worm bin. And we haven't even got to the critters that you can see really easily yet!

So let's take another step up the size chain and see what other creatures may be visiting or moving into your wormery.......

Potworms

You may at first mistake these for baby worms from your wormery stock, but in fact they are a totally different type of minute earthworm that lives in boggy ground. They are tiny white worms that will be a great benefit to your worm bin as they speed up the process considerably by eating the decomposing waste. Their own bodily waste then adds to the mix in the bin. Yes, your wormery is in effect one huge toilet! It isn't as bad as it sounds though, and as long as conditions are good and plenty of oxygen is present in the compost, it won't smell bad.

If you or your neighbours keep fish, try picking a few of these tiny worms out and feeding them to the fish as a treat. They are usually devoured greedily.

Ants

You don't want ants in your pants, and you certainly don't want them in your wormery either, well not in any great numbers anyway. Most wormeries that are sold in the UK are susceptible to ants as they can enter through the gaps at the sides of the trays, and ants search far and wide for anything edible. More than likely the only ants that you will see inside your bin are a few opportunist garden black ants hunting for an easy meal – but don't worry, worms are not on the menu. If they do discover something tasty though, you are soon likely to have a long trail of ants streaming backwards and forwards in a line between your bin and their nest, following a trail of pheromones left by the first visitors. They don't do any real harm, but can be an inconvenience when you are working on your wormery. If your wormery is raised on legs, the solution is simple – pop a can or empty ice cream container under each leg and fill it with water. Despite their many other amazing attributes, ants can't swim so those inside your bin that are now cut off from their nest will soon die, and no more can get in. If your wormery does not have legs I'm afraid that the only way to keep the ants out is to either relocate the bin, persuade the ants to move away, or wipe them out, something that I don't like doing. Follow the route march back to the nest and dust some ant powder outside the entrance. They will very quickly carry it inside the nest and feed it to the young, and the colony will die. Don't use ant powder, or any other insecticide for that matter, near your wormeries in case any gets carried inside. Remember, you are not just protecting your worms, but the entire micro-civilisation upon which they rely. If you don't like killing ants, there is a nematode that they don't like – simply water it around their nest and they will move away. Alternatively, try dusting with cinnamon or coffee powder, both of which they are apparently not keen on, and they should quickly move away.

If the ants actually move into your wormery to nest, then that is an entirely different matter. It will only be caused by one thing – your wormery is too dry. As the majority of wormeries are moist, this is very unlikely to happen. During prolonged hot weather, however, or if you have overdone the shredded paper and cardboard, conditions might just be suitable for a cosy formicary. Certainly I have had an ants nest in my normal garden composting bin – you know the ones, they look like plastic daleks. I took the lid off one day and a magnificent anthill had appeared on top of the rotting rubbish. I wasn't at all bothered and so left the millions of new residents in peace. You wouldn't want it happening in your worm bin though - not that black ants do any harm to your worms, but they would be very inconvenient.

The cure is very simple – use a watering can to lightly sprinkle the compost each day for a few days, and dig around in the contents with a hand fork. Ants don't like having all their egg chambers wrecked and so will soon move out.

Red ants are a different matter altogether. There is a good likelihood that red ants, especially the big red wood ants, may regard your worms as food. They may also give you a painful sting when you are working on your wormeries. They don't sting you in the way that a wasp or bee would, but spray a jet of formic acid, which is highly irritating to the skin. I've never had problems with red ants in my domestic wormeries so far, but if I did, then I think I would swallow my ethical qualms and destroy their nest. I've had nests of both types in my normal compost heaps on my allotments. I break them open with a garden fork or spade and leave them – the robins soon move in and make a meal of the eggs and grubs.

Mites

Red Spider Mites are the pests that leave cobweb-like threads all over your pot plants on the windowsill, or worse still on the tomatoes in your greenhouse. You won't find any in your wormeries as they like hot dry conditions, but they have plenty of distant relations that enjoy the moist atmosphere in your worm bins and luckily they are friends rather than pests. They feed on anything rotting, and sometimes on smaller creatures, as well as fungi and mould.

Flies

The commonest flies to get into your bins will be fruit flies, tiny black specks that erupt in a swarm when you open the lid. If your wormery is not a sealed system you will get them, no doubt about it, whether it is indoors or outside. They are the reason that I recommend a sealed system for indoor use, as infesting your house with them probably isn't high on your agenda. They are attracted to rotting fruit and vegetables in large numbers to drink the liquid exuding from the mix, and lay their eggs on the surface of the compost. They don't actually do any harm unless you manage to breathe one in as you lean over your wormery, and are part and parcel of the ecology of a compost heap, but they can drive you up the wall. If you really decide you've had enough, spread a layer of shredded paper, leaf mould or soil over the surface of your bin contents. This will stop the flies getting in to lay eggs, and prevent the hatchlings from taking wing to start the cycle all over again.

There are several other species of tiny flies that might infest your worm bin, but I tend to just call them all fruit flies. The treatment is the same, whatever type they are.

Even a sealed system indoors may get infested with flies, as there could be eggs laid in the kitchen waste before it is added to the wormery, especially if you store it in an open tub.

So what's next up in size?

Well if you are very lucky it might be one of these:

Pseudoscorpions

To be honest you are very unlikely to see one of these in your bin, or even in your large outdoor compost heap, despite the fact that there are no less than 26 species living in Britain. Very few people have ever seen them, due to their secretive nature and small size. I mention them only in passing in case you do stumble across one and think that you have venomous scorpions living with your worms! These tiny creatures only reach about 4mm in length, but if you look very closely you will see that they don't have the stinging tail that we all associate with true scorpions.

"I don't care if it doesn't have a sting – 'YOU' tell it to clear off!"

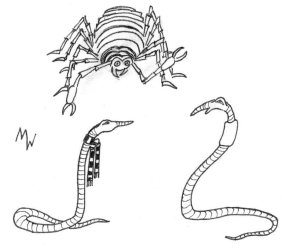

Worms and Wormeries

In fact you would probably mistake one for a spider, which is unsurprising as they are members of the arachnid family. Although they don't have a stinging tail, they do have venom – one of their front claws has been adapted into a stinger and injects venom when it nips tight. Don't worry though, they are harmless to humans.

The only true scorpion that we have in Britain is confined to the area around Sheerness docks in Kent, and even that species can only give humans a sting that is no more than a pin prick.

Springtails

One day you will be working in your wormery and when you disturb it, tiny white flea-like creatures will jump in all directions. Don't worry, you won't start scratching – these tiny residents are collembolan, commonly known as springtails on account of the forked tail that enables them to leap up to five times their length. They are very welcome residents in any wormery as they do a great deal of good, helping to speed up the rotting process. They can be a little alarming as they breed fast and live in huge numbers, but unless your wormery is indoors they don't pose a problem.

Wasps and Bees

Although I have had Bumble Bees nesting in my compost heaps on the allotments, it is extremely unlikely that either they or wasps would nest in a wormery as it is far too moist for them. Wasps may well be attracted to the smell of rotting fruit though, and become a nuisance if your wormery trays are of the open type. Burying the waste, as already detailed for flies, may well be enough to make them lose interest, but if they are persistent then trap jars may be needed. Punch a quarter inch hole in a jam jar lid, and quarter fill the jar with water. Add a tablespoonful of jam and stir it well. Screw the lid back on and stand the jar near you wormery. Wasps smell the jam, enter the jar and feed, which makes them drunk and they fall in the water and drown. If there is a nest nearby you can end up killing hundreds of wasps in a day or two. It is, however, a matter of debate as to whether the trap actually attracts more wasps than you would normally have had visit.

Millipedes

The armoured division have moved in when the millipedes arrive. Each black armoured segment of their bodies has four legs marching along below it, but they move quite slowly.

Visitors - The Good, the Bad and the Ugly....

You can't really see their legs from above, so they seem to glide along. Millipedes are vegetarian, eating anything that is decomposing, so they are useful in a wormery. There are usually quite a few of them in my allotment compost heaps, but I have yet to see one make it up into one of my tray wormeries in the garden – I suspect that they are not good climbers.

Centipedes

More of the armoured battalions, but it isn't quite so obvious in centipedes. A centipede's legs are to the side of their bodies, and they move very fast indeed; just try taking a photo of one! I had a lot of empty frames or photos of the last two or three sections before I finally managed to get this one.

Centipedes are carnivorous and eat just about anything that they can manage to kill with their venomous front claws. This could include your precious worms, so I prefer to turf them out of the wormery if I find any. You can safely pick them up, as they can't hurt you, but only if you can catch them!

Worms and Wormeries

Curiously, from a vegetable grower's point of view, millipedes are the enemy whilst centipedes are friends (slugs are amongst their prey), but when it comes to the wormery this situation is reversed.

Woodlice

There is no mistaking a woodlouse, as they are quite distinctive, but did you know that there are at least 37 different species in the UK?

No, neither did I. In fact I had to look it up. But I did know that there are two very distinct types – ones that can roll up into a ball, and ones that can't.

Their segmented shells resemble an armadillo, and in fact one genus is named Armadillidium – these are the ones that can roll up into a ball, hence one of their common names, pill bugs.

Woodlice are most welcome in a wormery as they feed on just about any rotting organic material. I currently have an adapted wheelie bin on my allotments that is set up as a wormery, and it is absolutely swarming with woodlice. When I set it up, I started it off with a good big load of well rotted goat manure that had been standing out in the open, and there were evidently plenty of woodlice eggs in it.

Slugs and Snails

These are the heavyweights of the bin invaders as some can grow to quite mammoth proportions. Personally I think that the huge brown slugs that look like a dollop of dog muck crawling across your lawn are just about the most repulsive creature that lives on our shores. I often find them on my allotments, and they make a satisfying squelch when stamped on by a wellie boot! If this sounds cruel, then I apologise, but slugs and vegetable growing do not mix, and at least it is an instant death. They serve no useful purpose as even my chickens won't eat them. Hugh Fearnley-Whitingstall recently tried to cook some on his tv programme as he was determined to find a use for them, but even he gave up and said they were awful. I admit that only a few slug species are actually gardening pests, but I can't tell the difference so I'm afraid that they all meet a similar fate. The same applies to common garden snails, although their demise is even more satisfying as they crunch rather than squelch! I don't kill other varieties of snail, however, as I am aware that some of them are quite rare - the Roman, or Edible Snail is now protected, because it is, well, edible, and too many were getting collected for the kitchen. Some are actually rather pretty too, like the stripey White Lipped Snail, which doesn't actually have white lips, just a white lip to the edge of its shell.

All slugs and snails should be removed from your wormery as soon as you spot them. Although they don't actually do any harm in your bin, quite the reverse in fact, they are likely to get trapped as they grow, and will eventually be in the bottom bin that you harvest and spread around your vegetables, and you don't really want to be spreading slugs eggs as well, do you?

Whenever I pull back the plastic covers on my conventional compost heaps, hordes of snails can be found clinging to the underside. In the winter there can be hundreds!

So there you have it: a great mix of seething wildlife, all growing, dying, rotting, eating, excreting and being eaten, with the majority of it taking place on such a small scale that you can't even see it. Most of it is beneficial as it creates the perfect habitat and food supply for your worms. Don't be alarmed at the prospct of a zoo moving into your back garden because, as I have already mentioned, most of the bigger creatures listed above won't put in an appearance in a well-designed sealed worm bin. I've included them primarily because some of them will certainly get into the more open large scale wormeries that I shall be dealing with later.

The Changing Seasons.....

You wouldn't go outside in January wearing a lightweight short sleeved shirt, shorts and sandals and feel very comfortable for long, would you?

No, of course not!

Now think about your worms. Is it reasonable to expect them to feel comfortable all the year round in the same set up? Again, the answer is no.

This is where you have some decisions to make. If you have a wormery sitting in a shady sheltered spot in the corner of the garden, the average cycle within that bin will be something like this: during the spring the worms will become active, feeding on the waste in the bin. As the weather gradually warms up, breeding activities will begin and your wormery will swing into full production. When it becomes really hot during the summer breeding will be at its peak unless the bin becomes too hot or dry – remember that worms need a lot of moisture for their day-to-day living requirements, including the mating act. As long as your wormery is shaded and you dampen it down a bit if need be, breeding will reach a crescendo and the worms will be devouring your kitchen waste at a quite spectacular rate.

As the days shorten and the temperature drops the worms will become less active, and when it drops much below the magical 20 degrees Celsius figure, all mating will stop. The worms will gradually eat less food and become semi-dormant.

When the temperature drops towards freezing point just staying alive becomes very difficult for worms living in a wormery. At a few degrees below freezing point for any length of time they will die. Why is this? Well, in the wild the worms would dive deep to avoid the frozen ground. If they can get a couple of feet below the rock hard surface they have a chance of survival, and although food is scarcer down at that level, there is enough to sustain them whilst their metabolism is slowed right down.

Now consider the worms in your wormery. On average the trays are a couple of feet long by about a foot wide and maybe nine inches deep, with only six inches of that being compost. So, when the temperature starts dropping, Willy the worm dives down and Clunk! He hits the bottom. Either that or Splash! He ends up in the sump.

The compost and waste within a plastic wormery is very damp, and it will rapidly start to freeze solid. Poor Willy can no longer move through it and is effectively "frozen in" or, as is more likely, he is frozen solid. If Willy has more than the average number of worm brain cells he will head for the surface between the trays as a means of survival where he will slowly dehydrate or starve or to death - unless he freezes solid first.

It's a pretty awful picture isn't it? I'm sorry if it is too graphic for you.

Actually no, I'm not sorry. If you want to have the fruits of their labour for your benefit, you really have to learn to look after the worms that are in your care. A wormery on legs is vulnerable to the cold from all sides, plus top and bottom. The severe cold only has to penetrate a few inches on each side and the whole wormery is frozen solid.

If at all possible your wormeries should be out of the worst of the elements for the most severe of the winter months. This could be in the garden shed, in the conservatory or in any sort of outhouse – in fact anywhere away from the worst of the frost. If you have an outside boiler cupboard then you will have the potential to keep an active breeding wormery all year round.

We are lucky in most parts of Britain in that the really bad sub-zero weather spells rarely last more than a week or two, and they only occur when those nasty Siberians send us one of their weather systems.

Most of you will probably only keep one wormery, so it shouldn't be too much of a problem finding a sheltered winter home for it. I move all of my wormeries into my greenhouse during the coldest months, and when it gets really cold I light the paraffin greenhouse heater and keep it burning 24 hrs a day. My greenhouse isn't used during the winter as we have two large polytunnels on our allotments where we grow our winter crops, but even if you use your greenhouse for winter growing you should still be able to spare a corner for your wormery.

Even on a bitterly cold February day, with snow on the ground outside, I have checked my wormeries in the unheated greenhouse and there have been fat happy worms feeding at the surface of the waste.

Don't forget that a wooden shed, and possibly even a brick built outhouse, may well not be frost proof, and a greenhouse certainly isn't. Unless you are providing artificial heating, further measures will be needed. The simplest method of all is to wrap your wormery up in a nice thick layer of bubble wrap. The main stationery stores usually sell this in big rolls as padding for delicate items in the post, and it is really simple to wrap it around your wormery and tie it in place. Try to cover the bottom too, but make sure that you don't cover the precious air holes in the lid or sides. It will only take a few moments to untie and unwrap when you need to gain access to inspect or work on the wormery. You should even be able to arrange things so that the lid can be removed without touching the bubble wrap. The simplest insulation for the top of the wormery is a deep layer of shredded paper on top of the kitchen waste. It can easily be scraped to one side if you need to add more food, and then replaced, and it will keep the worms very cosy. Some of my outside wormeries have survived a long really intensive cold spell with just a layer of shredded paper, so I know it works.

Depending on the size and shape of your wormery, other materials that may be used as insulation are polystyrene blocks, old carpets, cardboard (especially the rolls of corrugated cardboard that are sold for wrapping parcels) or even an old duvet. You can often pick up a duvet at a jumble sale or car boot sale for a pound or two.

If all of the above sounds like too much hard work, then perhaps you shouldn't be keeping a wormery. If your wormery is well established before the cold strikes it might well recover from being decimated, due to the hardiness of the many cocoons that will be buried in the compost. They may well hatch out and start the cycle off again, albeit very slowly, but you as a vermiculturalist (is there really such a word?) should do your very best to keep your wriggly charges safe and comfortable, both from a moral and practical point of view – you want the wormery to be maintaining production for as much of the year as possible.

If you have several wormeries, or they are too large to fit into the available space that you can keep warm, then you should make sure that you can at least keep one system operational. Move your smallest wormery indoors, or start a new one in the autumn using one of the home-made container ideas that I will discuss later. This way you can at least keep one colony alive and then restart the others once the severe weather has passed. If you don't, you may find yourself buying fresh stocks of worms every spring, particularly if you live in an area where harsh winters are normal.

The Fruits of Your Labour....

Well actually it's the fruits of your worms' labour, but you know what I mean. Most of the worms have vacated the bottom tray of your stacking system, you have used the harvesting bar in your flow-through wormery or you have tipped out the contents of a simple bin system and picked out the worms, ready to start again. Whichever system you use, you now have a nice big bucketful of this wonderful compost, and you can bung some in flowerpots and plant your flowers in it, can't you?

Wrong.

Er, Right?

Confused? I'm not surprised, as the entire world of worm composting seems to be somewhat confused! Some say that the finished product is too strong and will burn your plants, others state that it can be used neat with no harmful effects. We need to differentiate a little in order to clarify the situation.

Your wormery will definitely produce worm compost. This will be a lovely mix of worm cast and the decomposed remains of some of the kitchen waste that you have added. Depending on exactly what you have added, the amount and consistency of uncomposted debris will vary. The compost will be rich in active microbes, which have been proven to improve plant growth greatly. The plants definitely benefit from having these microbes around their roots.

If you have left your system rather too long before harvesting, or if you use a stacking system with several trays, then the finished product may well be pure worm cast, with very little organic material left in it. The few worms remaining will be getting rather hungry. Why only a few? It's simple really – if you are using multiple trays and maintaining them correctly the majority of the worms will have moved to where there is plenty of food. If an air gap has developed between the trays, thus stranding the worms, or you have left a single tray system too long, then they will have died off. The amount of available food, and living conditions, will always control the number of worms in any one tray or area of your wormery. The law of "the fittest survive" works very strongly in a wormery. The breeding rate also slows down significantly when food is scarce or the environment hostile. The pure worm cast that remains may be slightly acidic, and therefore alkaline-loving plants won't be too happy if you use it around them. Pure worm cast will also have lost much of its microbial content and the nutrient level will be reduced.

So why do some commercial breeders allow the worms to die off totally so that they produce pure worm cast? The answer is in the texture of the finished product, as it is a wonderful dark fine mix, similar to the rich soil of the fenlands of East Anglia. Its fine granules are ideal for mixing with other composts to produce the ideal mixture for use in seed trays and for potting on.

In the varied world of the vegetable gardener, both types of worm product are perfect. The only wormery where I insist on total worm cast production is in the dog poo bins, where I don't want to see any trace of the original organic material! Admittedly there may be traces of paper left, as I prefer to add a lot of it to these bins, but of the original dog poo there should be no sign. I am definitely not about to go picking through it for worms.

However, in all cases this product is going to be just too valuable to use neat. Unless you are worm farming on a big scale, realistically you are only going to get a tray full of compost or castings every couple of months, at best. All worm "experts" advise you to use worm compost as quickly as possible in order to make use of the live microbes. If stored, much of their value is lost. In my experience this isn't an issue – the stuff gets used up much too quickly to need to store it! I always have something growing somewhere on the allotments that will benefit from some compost, no matter what the season. I simply sieve the larger pieces of uncomposted waste out and return them to the top tray to continue breaking down, and use the rest on whatever the current growing project is.

Some compost is used neat as a top dressing around growing vegetables and fruit bushes. This has multiple benefits. The mulch effect of the compost deters weed growth around my precious plants, weed growth that would steal nutrients; the high humus content retains the soil moisture, helping to prevent the area drying out in hot dry periods; every time that it rains or you water, the compost releases nutrients that are washed down to the roots of the plant on a slow steady basis and finally, the microbes released "seed" the surrounding soil as they spread out. The compost can hold up to three times its own weight in water, which is a HUGE advantage when you garden in light sandy soils like mine, and it holds the water well so that you have to water less often.

All the above benefits can be greatly boosted by mixing your worm compost with other composts. You could use a commercial compost mix – it would certainly be improved by adding your worm compost – or you could produce your own compost mix.

I am fortunate in that the local council where I live deliver huge quantities of fallen leaves onto our allotments in late autumn. They are collected from the nearby streets and parks by a chap using a small tractor that has "vacuum cleaners" fitted underneath which suck up the leaves and blow them through pipes into a large caged trailer towed behind. The leaves are quite compacted and a normal trailer load can easily be a couple of tons, sometimes more. That's a lot of leaves! They are a mix from just about every variety of tree that grows in this country, although oak and sweet and horse chestnut prevail.

I have built a leaf pen on one of my plots, using very heavy duty plastic netting on three sides, which stands about three feet high. The fourth side is conventional wire netting which I stretch into place once the pen is full. When the trees have shed their leaves in autumn the tractor man trundles round to my plot, reverses up, and dumps load after load of leaves into my pen. If it is empty to start with it can easily take ten loads – which amount to twenty or more tons of leaves. I then spread some heavy netting over the whole thing to keep the leaves in place if we have any gales, and forget about it.

My leaf pen is topped up each year. As they decompose the level gradually drops and last years leaves are shovelled to one side to make room for the new season's delivery.

Some of the fresh leaves are used as litter in my chicken houses and runs. They break down, mix with uneaten greens and chicken droppings, and make a great addition to my wormeries and compost heaps when dug out once a year.

After a year the leaves in the leaf pen have begun to break down and I use them as a surface mulch around my vegetables. My soil is very light, so they help to retain moisture and keep down weeds.

A year later and they have really started to break down and can be rotavated into the vegetable beds in spring, together with plenty of manure from horses and chickens.

By the third year they have turned to a lovely rich golden brown soil. Mix this 50:50 with worm compost and in my opinion you have the best seed compost that you can find anywhere!

"So you see, Jenkins Junior, the humans go to a lot of trouble to make chemical fertilisers, when our natural products are so much better...."

My conventional compost heaps now get benefits from my wormeries as well. A lot of the weeds from my plots are fed to the chickens, but plenty still go into my compost heaps. I try to ensure that only weeds that have not flowered are used, to try to prevent my compost being full of weed seeds. Cauliflower, cabbage and Brussels sprout stalks go in there too, together with cut down raspberry canes, bean stalks and stems and a host of other allotment waste. I generate far too much waste for my wormeries to be able to deal with it all, so I have conventional compost heaps dotted around my plots, made up from old pallets. Quite frankly I don't have the time to keep turning them as you are supposed to, so they don't get hot enough to kill any weed seeds present.

When I dig them out to use the compost there are always some worms in amongst it, but not many. There is a host of other wildlife present including voles, frogs, toads and field mice. Once there was even a hibernating hedgehog. I'm sure that the reason for not many worms is because the tall heaps are just not moist enough for them, even with a lot of plant foliage added. The decomposition in my heaps is 99% due to microbe activity rather than anything else, and they take a long time to rot down. Generally I have to leave them a couple of years before digging them out for use. In a normal garden compost heap this decomposed matter would contain little in the way of goodness to improve soil, apart from increase the humus content, which is vital for water retention. I have always been lucky as I have chickens and, until recently, goats. Their manure has helped greatly to improve the quality of my compost. Since I have had wormeries this situation has changed dramatically for the better.

Initially I used the diluted sump contents to water my vegetables, especially my tomatoes, and I have to admit that the results were good. I don't think it is coincidence that I had bumper crops whilst suffering no blight at all. However, as my knowledge grew, I realised that some of the fluid in the sump is really quite nasty stuff and probably not really suitable for feeding to my vegetables. As the whole reason for us growing our own food is that we want to know what has gone into it, and we refuse to use chemicals or pesticides in any form, the unknown element in wormery sump juice made me feel uneasy.

I realised that there are actually two types of sump juice. Yes, I know, it's confusing! Let me explain.....

If your wormery has a waterproof lid or is totally under cover, then the juice that drains through the system will be extremely concentrated, consisting of decomposed kitchen waste juices and the excreta of the millions of creatures living there, all flushed through by the water that condenses inside the lid of a plastic wormery. This is pretty strong stuff; dark and smelly and swarming with anaerobic bacteria. They must be anaerobic as there can be little oxygen in stagnant water.

My first wormeries had small ventilation holes in the lids, and after heavy rain the sump would be full. This fluid would be much paler and didn't smell too bad unless any worms were decomposing in it.

The dark juice in a waterproof wormery takes quite a while to start collecting, at least two or three months if you are adding plenty of shredded paper or cardboard to the waste, whilst that washed through by rainfall can appear almost immediately.

I realised that this rain flush-through was what I had been using on my tomatoes. As I now check and drain the sump in my wormeries weekly, and the day after any heavy rainfall, I now use the juice in two separate ways.

The concentrated juice from a sealed wormery is now poured onto my conventional compost heaps and it certainly seems to speed up the decomposition process in them, especially if used on a freshly started heap. I would imagine that the juice has the same effect as the compost accelerators that you can buy from gardening shops.

I'm pleased to have found a good use for this juice as I believe that nothing should go to waste.

Juice flushed through by rainfall is still used to water my vegetables, and I dilute it further with water from my water butt. I generally use it at around four parts water to one part juice. I always use it immediately, as I believe that it may contain useful live bacteria that may be beneficial to my plants, and that these will be lost if stored and used later. I have to confess that I have no scientific fact to prove this, just a gut feeling.

A neighbour of mine on the allotments uses comfrey as a fertiliser. He chops a load up and drops it into a butt of water and leaves it for a few weeks. I first found out about it when I thought some large animal had died on his plot, as the smell drifting from it was terrible! He is producing his own liquid fertiliser, which he swears by, and says it is wonderful stuff.

I am now cultivating my own little comfrey patch to give it a try.

My parents used to grow their own vegetables. Whenever they had the opportunity to acquire some horse manure they would collect it up and take it home. This was stuffed into an old pair of tights and suspended in a water butt. A few days later and they had their own liquid plant feed.

Why am I mentioning all this in a book about worms? Well, quite simply, it gave me the idea to try something similar with worm cast. If the rainwater flushing down through the wormery was producing this wonderful fertiliser, how good would it be if I added worm cast or worm compost to water? The answer is that it is superb!

Simply fill a bucket with cold water, place a couple of handfuls or so of compost into an old stocking, suspend the stocking in the water, and leave it for a couple of hours. It will look as though you have brewed a bucket full of tea, and in fact this dark brown soup is often referred to as worm tea. Other books call the juice in the wormery sump worm tea as well though, so be careful that you don't get confused. Worm tea isn't really a wonderful name for any of it, in my opinion, as it conjures up images of an infusion of dried and shredded worms! In my own mind I separate them out as sump juice, rainwater juice, and brewed juice, although really there is little difference between the products of the last two.

If you are going to use your brewed juice in a watering can with a rose fitted, you will have to strain the juice again, as the suspended particles in it will block the rose holes. It's easier to remove the rose. In fact, if you are going to use the brew around trees and shrubs it isn't even really necessary to use a stocking when soaking compost in water. You can just add the compost to the water, and then carefully pour the finished brew around your plants. The compost that empties with the water will form a surface mulch that will slowly release yet more nutrients.

As I proved at the beginning of the book, the finished worm compost is a revelation when used in a weed-infested environment. Under normal circumstances I sow seeds on the plots on my allotments and within a couple of weeks they are a weed-choked mess. It is difficult to use a hoe because I can't see seedlings produced by the seeds that I have sown. In the past, more often than not, I have had to resort to tedious hand weeding – carefully pulling individual weeds out by hand, which is time consuming and back breaking! All this has changed since I started producing worm compost.

First of all I mix my worm compost 50:50 with well rooted leaf mould, thus doubling the amount of compost that I have available.

I then prepare my seed drill in the normal way, using a hoe to draw soil away to produce a long straight shallow trench at the depth that I need to sow my seeds. The seeds are sown at intervals along the trench, and then the trench is filled with the worm compost mix. As the seeds are only planted at half an inch to an inch deep, and the trench is only an inch or so wide, this does not use up a huge amount of compost.

Larger seeds that need to be planted deeper are treated slightly differently. The seed drill is prepared as above, but then individual holes are made to the correct planting depth using a wooden dibber, and a seed popped into each hole. The trench is then filled with worm compost mix, as above.

This might sound a bit time consuming and unnecessary, but you haven't yet heard the brilliant outcome of following this procedure.

When you have finished sowing, the rows of planted seeds stand out clearly because the worm compost is so much darker than the surrounding soil. Two weeks or so later the difference is even more astounding: The soil between the rows will almost certainly have been covered in a green fuzz of weed growth. The seed drills will stand out as rows of virgin soil, with little or no weed growth. If your seeds were of a quick growing variety there will be healthy young seedlings showing at regular intervals along the row. It is simplicity itself to hoe away the weeds without damaging any of your precious plants, which is considerably faster than laborious hand weeding and easier on the back. Even if weed seeds do eventually break through the worm compost barrier and emerge, my vegetable seedlings have a strong head start and it is easy to distinguish them from weeds, and only a few moments work to walk along a row and pull out offenders.

Throughout the next few months, every time it rains or you water the plants, the nutrients from the worm compost in the seed drill will be washed down to their roots, promoting healthy and vigorous growth – exactly what you want in your vegetables.

Pot plants in your home will also benefit from the addition of worm compost, especially as the soil in a pot will become very tired and lacking in nourishment over time. Some pot plants live for many years and unless fed regularly their growth will become stunted and flowering is often diminished. Adding some worm compost every couple of months will give them a new lease of life and save you the expense of buying plant food. Simply scrape out the top inch of old soil from around your pot plant and replace with worm compost.

A word of warning here – there is a possibility that the compost you use in your plant pot on the windowsill might contain the eggs of some creepy crawlies. This usually isn't a problem as they will live happily in the soil for a while and then die, but if it is fruit flies that hatch out they could be a bit annoying. Their numbers are sure to be tiny, but if you think it might be a nuisance, the best bet is to kill anything in the compost before adding it to your pots. By far the easiest way to do this is to place your compost in a glass bowl and then zap it in the microwave for a couple of minutes. That will do the trick.

Moving on to Bigger Things....

No, I don't mean crossing slow worms with garden worms to create a superworm!

The vast majority of people who are reading this book will only be interested in running a small wormery, probably one of the manufactured models, to make good use of their kitchen waste to produce some useful compost.

Some of you may be interested in trying out a wormery, but are reluctant to spend a lot of money until you've tried it out to see how you get on with running one.

Some of you will be wanting to do things on a grander scale, possibly because you have horses or other large livestock and need a good way of disposing of their waste, or because (like me) you want to produce that lovely compost on a larger scale to enhance your vegetable and/or fruit growing.

The good news is that there are do-it-yourself home made options to please all of you. In fact there is no real need to ever buy a wormery from a retailer if you don't want to, although I do believe that if you only intend to run one or two small wormeries you would probably do better to do so. Without a doubt, professionally built wormeries are more pleasing to the eye than many of the home-made jobbies, but the important thing is that we all get composting, however we do it. "Slim your bin" is a campaign slogan used by councils throughout East Anglia in an attempt to get us to cut down the amount of waste going into landfill sites. Composting your kitchen waste will be taking a big step towards this aim, so it doesn't matter what your wormery looks like – the fact that you are running one is the important thing. Certainly the two largest home-made wormeries that I will be telling you about would be better situated at the bottom of your garden rather than outside your window.

Provided that your worms have food, oxygen, warmth, darkness and a damp environment that doesn't turn anaerobic or drown them, they will probably live quite happily for years and build up their numbers at a fast rate. I have successfully sometimes kept them in plastic cartons measuring 15″ long by 12″ tall by 8″ deep that previously held building plaster – obviously well cleaned out before using!

Worms and Wormeries

Plenty of holes punched around the top of the sides and a few in the bottom and they make a good mini-wormery that can be kept in a corner of a shed or garage. If your wormery population is getting rather full but you don't have another wormery free to move some into, then a large tub can be a standby overspill home until you are ready. Stand the tub on several sheets of newspaper to absorb any juices rather than have a pool form in your shed, and change the paper from time to time. When you change the paper don't forget to place the discarded paper in one of your wormeries!

A step up from this is the many types of plastic boxes sold for under-the-bed storage. Some of them are absolutely ideal for creating small wormeries, especially those that have lids. Simply treat them in much the same way as shown above. If they are semi-transparent plastic you can get round the daylight problem by finding a cardboard box that the storage box will fit inside – cut the bottom out of the cardboard box and slip it over the plastic box like a sleeve so that it acts as a cover.

If you want to be really inventive look for some of the coloured plastic storage boxes (usually with no lids) that stack inside one another. A couple of hours work with a drill making hundreds of holes in the bottoms of all the boxes except one (to use as a sump tray), and you have the trays for a stacking system wormery. Drill ventilation holes around the tops of all the sides in all of the boxes, including the sump and, if the top box has a lid, then you are ready to go. If not then a lid can easily be made from a sheet of stiff plastic or metal, or if the wormery is going to be kept in a shed or garage, then even a sheet of cardboard will do the job.

A luxury model can be constructed by fitting a tap as low as possible in the sump (plastic taps that fit home brewery fermenting bins, or those made for water butts, are ideal) and using another storage box upside down at the bottom as a base to raise the whole thing off the floor so that you can use the tap.

A complete working tray system wormery – probably for less than twenty quid!

Another good starter bin is a plastic dustbin. They can be bought quite cheaply and all that is needed is some hole drilling. Contrary to what some books advise, don't drill the lid. Keeping it whole will prevent rainwater flushing through your wormery. As the bin won't have a sump, you don't want to lose the nutrients that would be leached out by heavy rain. Drill holes all round the top edge of the bin itself for ventilation, and in the base for drainage.

Moving on to Bigger Things.....

The bin will need to be tipped out when you harvest the compost, and the worms picked or sieved out. Ideally, you should stand the working bin permanently wherever you will be doing the tipping, as it will be very heavy when full and very difficult to move.

Progressing up from dustbins, I have a full-sized wheelie bin on my allotments that works quite well as a wormery. I grabbed one when the allotment shop were selling off old ones for use as water butts.

Keeping chickens and goats on allotments is quite difficult during the harshest winter months as the water supply is switched off to prevent pipes freezing and bursting. It is difficult to manually take enough water with you, so I settled on a jerry can full of hot water for thawing out all the drinkers in the chicken runs, and for watering the goats – goats will not drink cold water, whilst the chicken's drinkers were refilled with water stored in the wheelie bin, which was itself stored in the polytunnel to keep the water from freezing.

When we sold the goats I was left with an unused wheelie bin – and promptly converted it into a wormery. It isn't ideal, but it does work.

I fitted it with a drainage tap, an old one from a spare home brew fermentation bin, but I couldn't get it particularly low down because of the slightly curved front of the bin. It is probably four inches above the lowest inside bin level. I got round this by filling the bottom of the bin with large cobblestones dug up from my plots to a depth of about six inches.

I then inserted a layer of weld mesh over the stones, and added a good thick layer of broad bean stems and foliage to form a mat. This was topped with a layer of shredded paper, and then I added the worms complete with a good nesting bed of their own vermicompost.

I drain the bin regularly by tipping it forward with the tap open. It obviously doesn't empty it completely but if any worms are unfortunate to fall into the drain area, they can at least crawl back up via all the cobblestones. I have no way of telling if any perish, but I doubt it, and the worm population remains high. There are no air holes - as the bin is so tall, I feel that there is plenty of air trapped inside and I empty it when three quarters filled. I'm sure that if I tried to fill it completely the sheer weight of the compost would cause the lower levels to become so compressed that anaerobic conditions would be inevitable. This bin is so big that it is impossible to move even when only partially full. The wheels just sink into the ground and it bogs down. It is permanently positioned in a sheltered spot beside one of my sheds, where it can simply be tipped forward to empty it when it is harvesting time. I have a wheelbarrow handy, and shovel the top foot of waste and worms into the barrow, and then tip the bin over.

After sorting through and picking out the cobblestones and wire mesh, I set it up to start again and refill it with the contents of the wheelbarrow.

Most of the worms are in the top twelve inches of waste that I remove and replace into the new set-up.

This type of bin, that is deep but has only a small surface area, is more prone to becoming anaerobic if not carefully managed. I make sure that I add plenty of shredded paper regularly, as well as other woody material such as chopped up raspberry canes. A lot of this doesn't decompose very well, but I am not too bothered as I simply rake the tipped out bin contents to remove the debris, and uncomposted bits and pieces are dropped back into the bin to continue decomposing.

Incidentally, this bin stands out in all weathers and recently survived a three week long spell of temperatures below minus five degrees Celsius. The only protection it had was a three inch layer of shredded paper on top of the waste, and its sheltered position kept it out of the bitingly cold wind.

Although it works I couldn't really recommend this system as it needs a lot of care to keep it running smoothly. I mention it only to highlight that, with a bit of imagination and careful husbandry, there are many unlikely-looking containers that can be turned into a wormery.

If you are at all handy at DIY, a satisfactory worm bin can be constructed from a single sheet of 8′ x 4′ half inch plywood, which in today's "new money" is 2400mm x 1200 mm x 18mm.

The reinforcing framework can built from any timber around 1″ x 1″ in size, screwing and gluing the joints for extra strength.

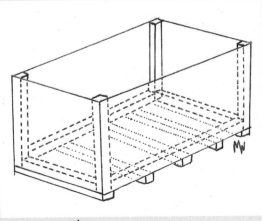

Centring at 1½" from the top, drill 1" holes at intervals around the sides, and drill ½" holes in the ends at the corners, as close as possible to the bottom. The lift-off lid is completed by screwing pieces of timber around the underside edges to act as an overhanging lip to keep it in place.

Finish off by preserving the wood with a wood treatment that is safe for worms and allowing it to dry thoroughly before introducing the worms.

The outside can be treated or painted to give an attractive appearance. Because the wood is constantly in contact with damp compost, this system has a limited life, probably no more than 4 years if used continuously. This can be extended considerably if the wormery is emptied, allowed to dry out thoroughly, and then re-treated annually.

Your worms can be temporarily housed in one of the containers described above whilst their house renovations are in progress.

This worm box is strong enough to be used as a seat in your patio area, but be careful to avoid too much direct sunlight. Bear in mind also that it is likely to be far too heavy to move, so give some thought as to how you will protect it during cold weather. Its square shape lends itself well to polystyrene blocks, cut to size and tied in place around the sides, with another large block sitting on the lid – with a suitable weight on top of course.

When first starting off the worm box, place the worms' nesting material on the floor in the middle of the box and spread it out, but do not take it right to the sides. Cover with a thin layer of kitchen waste and perhaps some special delicacies that you know they will enjoy. By the time that the food and bedding has spread out to reach the sides and the worms discover the drainage holes, they are very unlikely to leave en masse as they will be settled and have a ready food supply. Worms generally only try to decamp from any wormery if there is no food or the conditions are bad. Being covered and of wooden construction with plenty of ventilation, this system is unlikely to sweat and produce excessive moisture, so the drainage holes should be sufficient. If for any reason there is not enough drainage, it is easy enough to drill more holes.

This system is used extensively in America, where they were composting using worms long before manufactured wormeries were available.

If you want to process a lot of material then you obviously need a much bigger waste-holding capacity. A good set-up can be made using old pallets. The best ones to use are printer's pallets that have a close boarded surface rather than conventional ones that have gaps between all the boards. Printer's pallets are also slightly smaller.

The size of your wormery really only depends on the room that you have available and the number of pallets that you can acquire.

Even so, it should never be more than six feet wide so that you can still get easy access to all areas from either side. The larger that you can make it, the easier it will be to empty when it is time to harvest, as you can climb in and still have room to use your shovel. The basic frame of the wormery is fairly easy to construct, but if you want to make it rat/mole/vole proof then a little more work is required.

Mark out the area that you are going to build on with pegs and string lines and dig out about six inches of soil within the marked space. Get this whole area level and check it by laying a long piece of timber down inside the hole and placing a spirit level on it. Check it across both diagonals and also lengthwise and dig it out until you get it right. Build your wormery frame by nailing pallets together with the boarded surfaces facing inwards. You may find that you have to hammer 2 x 2 inch posts in at one or two points to give support. If you place these at the inside corners they will strengthen the whole structure. You will end up with a four-sided wooden box perhaps two pallets wide by whatever the length that you have chosen.

Now for the pest prevention measures – you need to line the whole of the floor and about a foot up the insides with half inch chicken wire nailed in place. If your wormery frame is six feet wide, buy 4 foot wire and lay just over 3 feet lengthwise on the ground inside the frame and bend the rest up the side wall. Allow an extra twelve inches at each end so that this can also be turned up against the end walls. The corners have to be folded and flattened. Secure it all in place with a hammer and staples or use a heavy duty staple gun (much easier). When one side is finished do the other side with the wire overlapping down the centre of the floor. To be super-safe you can secure the overlapping wire together at intervals with plastic cable ties or wire.

Once finished, you can shovel the soil back in that you excavated, and smooth it out. That's the pests kept out, but now we have to keep the worms in. Use one or more sheets of woven black plastic sheeting to line your framework. This sheeting is sold in builders merchants and is intended for use under patios, decking, woodchip mulches etc. and is designed to allow water to pass through whilst preventing weed growth. I use it extensively on my allotments to cover plots when they are not in use to stop the weeds taking over. Do not use unwoven plain sheet plastic or your wormery will flood!

The soil that you replaced will form a padded barrier between the wire and the sheeting and prevent rodents from nibbling the sheet through the wire, which would create holes and allow worms to escape. Having made sure that the sheeting is flat all over the floor area and not stretched anywhere, bring the excess up and over the sides and secure it in place all round with batons nailed around the top inside edge.

The last stage is optional and depends upon your overall wormery size, but will make life much easier at harvesting time. Make a square wooden frame – it only needs to be 1″ x 1″ timber – that will fit inside your wormery from side to side and cover it with smallish gauge wire netting. Nail this frame in place, and repeat at intervals, according to the length of your wormery. The idea is to divide your wormery into sections, but allow the worms to migrate to where the food is located.

Start the worms off in an end section and keep adding waste as normal until the section is full, then start on the next one along. When that one is full start filling the next one, and so on. As the worms migrate along the length of the wormery following the food, sections that have been fully composted can be dug out and harvested. The wire partitions keep the contents of the next section in place rather than having to contend with a landslide. With this system you tend to get worm compost rather than pure worm cast as the worms are always moving, and few stay behind to completely exhaust the organic material. If you don't fancy the extra work involved in making partitions you can always use the harvesting methods described after my next wormery.

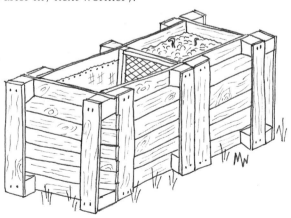

Worms and Wormeries

The finishing touch for your pallet wormery is a cover. The best one is a good thick carpet cut to fit inside the pallets, leaving about an inch gap all round. This will serve two purposes – keeping moisture in, and keeping birds out. The gap round the edge will discourage worms from trying to find a way out as they will avoid the daylight. If you are using the wire netting section dividers, cut separate pieces of carpet for each section.

As most of this structure is above ground, as with all raised beds natural drainage plus the strong winds and sun may make it a much drier environment than other wormeries, and so it may need to be lightly watered with a watering can or hose during dry spells. For me in dry East Anglia this means throughout most of the summer!

The most you can expect to get out of this wormery is about 5 years as pallets in contact with damp soil equals rot. If you thoroughly treat the pallets with preservative (something harmless to worms, obviously) and allow them to dry thoroughly before building, then you may extend the lifetime significantly. Mine was demolished as it was occupying space needed for a new polytunnel, and I have now moved over to a permanently mobile everlasting wormery – now that has got you wondering, hasn't it?

How do I achieve this? Well, I have discovered old baths. They are quite easy to source, as modern homeowners like to keep up with the latest fashions and styles in bathroom designs. Put word out among your friends, neighbours and relations, and if that doesn't work, enquire at your local council waste site or, probably best of all, approach a bathroom fitter – they are only too glad to get rid of the ones that they rip out! You don't want a cast iron bath as they are way too heavy. You are looking for one of the fibreglass ones. They usually come in some awful 1970's colours like avocado, dark blue or a dreadful brown. I'm currently using a pretty pink one and aim to add two or three more.

Due to their light weight when empty, they can be re-located between batches, if need be.

All you need to do is dig out a shallow hole the size and shape of your bath, and slightly sloping down at one end. Drop your bath into the hole with the plughole end at the bottom of the slope and shovel the excavated soil up against the sides to hold it steady. This uncomplicated wormery is now ready and the only expense involved is to buy a sink strainer – those things that fit over your kitchen sink plughole to stop food waste blocking the u-bend. They are very cheap and once fitted in the plughole of your bath, will stop your worms escaping.

Now you simply start the wormery off in the usual way by placing a layer of worm bedding in the bottom of the bath and adding your worms, and then add food waste at intervals to build the level up. Again make a cover from a piece of carpet and continue to fill with waste at intervals until it reaches about two inches blow the rim.

In order to harvest the compost you need a means of separating it from the worms. The easiest way is to stop feeding for a month. There will still be plenty of food present to keep the worms alive and healthy. After a month or so dig out a hole at one end, and spread this over the surface of the rest of the compost. Now fill the hole created with the choicest worm food that you can find. Use teabags, stale bread, pasta, worm treat – all their favourites. Scrape some compost back over this mix, and then leave for a couple of months. The majority of the worms will migrate into this area of plentiful choice food and you can dig the food out, complete with worms. As with my wheelie bin wormery, have a wheelbarrow handy as a place to deposit the worms and their bedding, harvest the compost in the bath and then return the worms and bedding to start afresh.

Always use a garden fork rather than a spade to dig out your worm nucleus as it is less likely to cause injury to your worms. You won't capture all the worms, but you will have enough to start the next colony. Any remaining in the compost will help to increase the worm population in your garden when you use the compost.

Another method I have seen is to make a cage out of wire netting or preferably weld mesh by cutting a broad cross shape, and then bending the arms of the cross up to form a basket. Use cable ties or wire to secure the corners. You then fill this basket with all the food goodies and sink it below the surface of the compost in the bath.

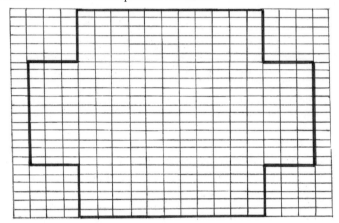

A couple of months later you simply lift it out, worms and all. It is probably less traumatic for the worms than being dug out.

The worm retrieval process has to be carried out at a time of year when the worms are fully active so that they migrate to the areas where you can collect them, so a little advance planning is needed.

Both the pallet wormery and the bath wormery are big enough to cope with horse manure, but don't add too much at once, and don't forget what I said earlier about allowing it to mature for a while before use. Manure needs plenty of carbon-based materials to be added regularly, so don't forget the shredded paper and cardboard, unless there is lots of hay or straw already in the mix.

These large wormeries are unlikely to be situated in particularly sheltered spots, so extra insulation is probably going to be needed during harsh weather. The easiest method is to position bales of hay or straw against all four sides. Sheets of bubble wrap can be laid on top of the carpet covers, the more layers the better. Place bricks or something else heavy at intervals to keep it all in place during windy weather. A good layer of hay or straw would do the job too – remove your carpeting, lay the hay on top of the compost, then replace the cover.

If you are troubled by larger wildlife, such as rats or badgers climbing up the sides of your wormery and attacking the contents from the top, or if you want to shelter your worms from heavy rain or excessive sunlight, you may need to build a solid cover. This can be achieved easily enough using half inch plywood. Cut the sheet to the size of your wormery, allowing a couple of inches extra all round. Nail 1″ x 1″ timber around the edge on the underside all round to form an overlap lip to keep the cover in position. The lid may need to be tied or weighted to keep it in place in high winds. The outside (top) of the cover can be painted or treated with preservative to lengthen its life as it will not be coming into contact with the worms. If your pallet wormery is very long the lid can be constructed in two or more sections to keep it to an easily manageable size.

An alternative maintenance method for these larger outdoor wormeries is the pocket-feeding system that I mentioned earlier in the section dealing with commercially made wormeries.

Mary Appelhof, the American pioneer of worm composting advocates pocket-feeding, and whilst I can't really see what it achieves in a small system, it may be useful in a larger wormery as it concentrates the worms into one area to make gathering them easier at harvesting time.

Basically it works by burying the food into a designated spot in your wormery, and the next time you feed your worms you bury it in the adjacent spot, and so on. The worms migrate through the soil, following the food. You draw up a plan for your wormery like this:

1	4	5	8	9	12	13
2	3	6	7	10	11	14

I have adapted the plan to suit the shape of a pallet or bath wormery. Starting in area 1, you bury your food just under the surface. The next feed is buried at 2 then at 3 etc. Unless you have an extremely good memory you have to keep a written record of the feed spots and dates. I cannot for the life of me see the point of running this system from day one as it seems a lot of work for no reward, but it can be very useful when you are nearing harvesting time. Once your system is three quarters full of compost, achieved by normal top feeding, leave it for a month or so without feeding and then start the pocket-feeding. By then the worms will be a bit peckish and will head for the buried food. This won't happen overnight as the waste will be too fresh, but it will soon begin to decompose and they will start feeding. Simple gardening name labels can be used, stuck into the surface of the compost, to keep a track of the feeding position. Label one "LAST FEED" and the other "PREVIOUS FEED," and move them along as you proceed. Next time you open the bin to add waste, you can see which direction you are moving in, so once you have buried the waste in the next spot, the PF label gets moved to the position of the LF, and the LF goes where you have just buried the food.

By leading the worms to one end of the bin, you can then harvest the compost from the remaining area. It is then a simple matter to spread the un-harvested compost (containing the worms) across the floor of the wormery and recommence top feeding. The compost will provide their bedding to start the system off again.

Both the pallet wormery and the bath tub wormery will deal with good quantities of waste, and even a certain amount of animal manure. However, if you have more than one horse or pig you will find that you need a far more efficient means of processing their copious waste products.

You could easily progress to a system that can be as large as the amount of waste that you have, provided that you have the space available. Serious equestrians are not normally short of a bit of land, so why not give this method a go – it involves no cost whatsoever, assuming that you are already running a garden wormery or two to provide your starting breeding stock.

Your initial manure must be partly composted naturally, to flush through the "hot" elements that are harmful to your worms.

You will require a strip of land about ten feet wide, and as long as you want to go, preferably tucked away out of sight as it will not make a pretty addition to your garden!

Simply spread your matured horse muck out on the ground in a strip about four to five feet wide by about six inches deep and however long you like. Water it well with a hose or can and then introduce your worms to their new home. You will need about a thousand worms for each foot of length – ie. 6000 worms for a six foot long starter strip.

Water the heap thoroughly at least twice a week – daily in really hot weather – and add another six inch layer of rotted manure on top every couple of weeks. When the heap reaches a couple of feet high you can start adding fresh manure to the end of the heap, extending it in a straight line. It is important to water frequently as a raised heap will dry out very quickly, especially in windy or hot conditions. There is no risk of flooding these types of wormeries as water is able to drain freely, although a certain amount of caution has to be exercised with heaps built on heavy clay soils.

By the time that the worms are ready to move across to the fresh manure, your frequent watering will have leached out the urine and other strong elements and it will be ready for consumption. When the heap reaches three feet high, stop adding manure and move on along the row. When you have achieved the desired length, simply deposit the manure in a u-bend turn, returning in the direction that you started with about a three feet gap between the stacks. Eventually you perform another u-turn and return to your starting point. Of course, there won't be a heap there to join up with as you will have long since harvested your massive heap of worm compost on a continuous basis.

The beauty of this system is that if conditions in the heap become hostile, for instance if it dries out, the worms can escape to either side into the surrounding soil. They won't travel far from this rich food source and will soon return when the heap becomes worm-friendly again. It is, however, a completely "open house" system where all manner of critters can become house guests. None are likely to harm your worm population to a great extent, even moles or shrews, as you will be operating with big worm numbers, so small-scale predation is unlikely to be noticed. There is no real need to form the oval-shaped heap as you can simply work in a straight line, and when you reach your limit, skim the top layer of compost, complete with worms, from your "working" end and return it to your start point. You then add matured manure and begin again. The loop system takes away the pressure on you to dig out the fully composted sections as it will be much longer before you reach that spot again, and it allows you to accumulate a sizeable amount of worm compost so that you are able to fertilise a large vegetable plot in one go instead of messing about with small quantities.

Some commercial worm farms operate in a similar way to this, sometimes using pits rather than heaps. Sometimes their heaps will be built on a fully concreted area to facilitate the use of large scale tractors and machinery. Some work with manure, or waste from a food processing plant such as fruit pulp. Others use brewery waste or spent mushroom farm compost. When our government or local councils finally get their act together, this will undoubtedly be the way in which large quantities of domestic waste will be recycled, rather than being dumped into landfill sites.

Moving on to Even BIGGER Things....

Okay, so you have been running your wormery in your garden for a while now, or maybe even progressed onto a larger home-made system, so now your mind is moving on to even bigger and better projects, possibly even to the point of wanting to earn a living from worm farming.

You may have seen exciting websites or magazine articles telling you that there is a shortage of worms and that there are queues of people wanting to buy your worms. Some companies promise to buy all the worms that you can produce. For a "small" investment of ten to fifteen thousand pounds you could be set up for life. There is even a government website advising you how to register your land as a worm farm, which adds apparent substance to the claims.

Blah blah!

But just think about it.....

Where are all these people falling over themselves to buy worms?

Fishing bait suppliers? Not really as maggots are still far more popular as bait in Britain.

Compost suppliers? Have you been into your local garden centre and bought a bag of worm compost? No, I thought not.

Home worm composters? Well yes, as the interest in composting kitchen waste grows there will certainly be more demand for worms, but this is usually only a one-off purchase of a small quantity of worms unless disaster strikes and you have to start again. I am pretty confident that the current number of worm farmers would be able to satisfy this demand.

Don't mistakenly believe that you will be able to sell enough packets of worms to new home composters to use the worms that you are producing – the schemes that I have seen involve breeding hundreds of tons of worms a year. A sign by your front gate advertising "Worms sold here" next to the one selling eggs isn't going to shift that many worms!

Some of the companies offering to set you up as a worm farmer, (and relieving you of large sums of money in the process) guarantee to buy back the worms that you produce. Some of these companies undoubtedly use your worms to set up other gullible people with their starting stock. Once they reach the stage of being inundated with worms from the numerous people that they have set up (in both meanings of the word) they disappear, the company folds, and they start again with a new name. Farmers who spent thousands of pounds on the equipment find themselves with no market for their product. Those who can't cope with running a worm farm may end up selling the equipment back to the supplier at a fraction of the price paid. The con merchant will have more equipment that he can offer to new prospective mugs at slightly reduced "bargain" prices as it has been used for "demonstration purposes" and the cycle begins again.

Think about it – if these schemes were so profitable would they be selling them to you? If I had a money-making machine I wouldn't sell its secrets to somebody else; I would build another machine myself and make even more money with it! The same applies to worm farms – if they were so good the existing establishments would be constantly buying new land themselves and farming larger and larger areas, eventually reaching the point where being unable to carry out all the work themselves wouldn't be a problem, as with all these immense profits they would be able to afford to hire staff to do the work for them, or at least the machinery to make the jobs quicker and easier.

Admittedly these large schemes are aimed at the existing farmer who has large amounts of land to spare and who is unlikely to be reading this book, but there are smaller scale scams also operating which make use of the age-old pyramid selling racket. They involve selling an initial home composting system and worms to a mug punter on the promise that they will be able to sell their worms on to other new people entering the market and earn a commission on selling equipment, and so on ad infinitum.

Another racket is charging you to subscribe to a newsletter that will give you the inside information on how to make a fortune from worm farming.

Another con I heard about in America involves a kind of adopt-a-worm scheme where the company sells you worms, but they keep them and breed them on their own premises, and then pay you the profit when they sell them. Of course when pay-out time arrives the company has disappeared and so has your money! I haven't heard of this racket being operated in the UK, but where America leads, the UK usually follows.

I wouldn't have thought that people would be gullible enough to fall for that one, but as the postal "You have won a prize but need to send money to register your claim" frauds seem to continue to catch greedy mugs, nothing surprises me any more.

All of these "too good to believe" offers promise big earnings, sometimes over one thousand pounds a month from worm farming, but the truth is that many of them are just that: too good to be true.

There are undoubtedly good honest companies out there that are operating in a legitimate manner, but how can you tell who they are? The simple answer is that you can't and a great deal of caution should be exercised before parting with any of your hard-earned cash, and talk to several companies. Ask to be put in touch with some of their customers who have been operating successfully for a long time. Don't settle for written references – contact the people direct and ask questions. A reputable company will not mind you checking them out, indeed they will know that you are genuinely interested and not a time waster.

If you really would like to expand your worm keeping you could always start small by selling worm compost from your front gate to test the response, and if it sells try finding your own market. For instance, most council allotment sites have a field shop, and perhaps they would be willing to sell your product. Word of mouth is a wonderful sales aid – if gardeners try your compost and have good results they will certainly tell others and your market will increase.

Try approaching local garden centres to see if they would be interested in selling bags of your wonderful compost. Go armed with proof of how effective the compost is, and be prepared to offer it to them on a sale or return basis so they have nothing to lose, but don't supply them with too much without getting paid as there are crooked garden centres about too. Don't bother trying big national chains – all their buying is done through their head office and the local shops have little say in what they stock.

Remember that if you do start selling to retail units they will expect a consistent supply and the compost will have to be properly bagged and labelled to comply with the law – "weight when packed" springs to mind as something important, because the weight will drop as the compost dries out inside a warm shop.

To quote those famous words of the sergeant in Hill Street Blues, "Let's be careful out there."

A ONCE IN A LIFETIME CHANCE!
(You certainly won't come back a second time)

MUG PUNTERS....sorry .... INVESTORS WANTED

INVEST IN WORM FARMING TODAY
– the new way to
GET RICH QUICK
(That's me, not you)

JUST £10,000 WILL GET YOU STARTED

Apply online today at
www.itsacon.com
email: mugs@itsacon.com

Bokashi Composting

"Blimey, what's he on about now?"

I can hear you thinking it, even from this far away.

I cannot finish a book about composting without mentioning a new composting method which is rapidly gaining an army of fans, and which fits in well with worm composting.

Worm composting is relatively new to most people in the UK, although it has actually been floating around for something like thirty years. It just hasn't "caught on" and become fashionable until now, but times are changing and many people are now realising the benefits of running a wormery at home, whether aimed at living a "greener" lifestyle or simply because they know it produces such superb compost/fertiliser.

Bokashi composting is something very new indeed, and it is sweeping around the world at speed. Several retailers in Britain are now selling bokashi kits and, unlike most wormeries, your bucket can sit in a corner of your kitchen or even in the cupboard under the sink. As it is a sealed system it is completely odourless and there is no danger of flies etc. invading your home. Bokashi can even process meat and fish without becoming smelly.

Yes, you did read that correctly, meat and fish, items that are taboo to a conventional compost heap or wormery.

It works on a very clever idea developed in Japan by Professor Teruo Higa. The original research was aimed at creating a method of increasing the number of microbes in the soil, but led to the development of the bokashi bin, which looks very much like a wormery bin.

Nothing could be simpler to use. You just tip your waste into the bin and cover it with a layer of specially activated bran. This bran and molasses mix has been seeded with a whole host of friendly bacteria, fungi and other microbial organisms which immediately start working on the waste and process it in just a couple of weeks. The best way to operate bokashi is to have two bins, one in the kitchen which you fill with your waste and one outside which is full and composting. When the kitchen bin is full you empty the fully composted outside bin and swap them over. The average home will take two weeks to fill a bin, and that is how long the full bin should be left for, so it works very well. The finished product doesn't look like conventional compost; if anything it looks more as though your kitchen waste has been pickled.

The treated waste can then be dug into your soil where it will quickly break down and provide humus when added to your garden composting system, or, and here is the good bit – fed to your worms.

The downside is that you have to buy fresh supplies of the bran regularly, but at the time of writing this book the cost only amounts to around three pounds a month, which isn't a bad price to pay for two big buckets of highly nutritious compost every month, all the year round.

Bokashi isn't subject to the vagaries of the British weather and would be particularly useful during the winter months when your worms may be semi-dormant and not processing much of your kitchen waste. Simply Bokashi the excess, and then feed it to your worms in the warm months when they may be working so fast that you can't provide enough food for them.

As a final plus point the buckets even have a tap to drain off fluid which, if poured into your drains, will keep them smelling fresh.

Amazingly you can even buy bokashi bran incorporated into layers' mash for chickens, which it is claimed is good for the chooks metabolism and also cuts down the smell from their droppings! If you have ever walked past a chicken run on a wet day you will know that this is a good idea!

Problem Solving at a Glance

My wormery smells awful when I remove the lid!

Assuming that you haven't fed your worms with meat, fish or dairy products, then you almost certainly have allowed the compost to become too wet and anaerobic bacteria have taken over.

Dig down into the compost and you are highly likely to discover a black slimy mess. If so you probably haven't added enough shredded paper/cardboard to the mix. If you are operating a single bin system, have you drained the sump area lately? If not the juice may have backed up and be flooding the lower levels of the wormery. In this case the best thing to do is to rescue what worms you have left (if any) and restart the system.

In a tray system, if it is the top tray that is affected, open up the compost with a hand fork, add plenty of shredded paper and cardboard and stir it all in. The worms don't normally like being stirred up, but in an emergency situation like this keeping them alive is more important than worrying too much about their temporary discomfort.

Dig around a bit every day for a couple of weeks, to keep opening up the compost and letting in air.

If it is a tray in the middle of the stack that is affected, simply remove it, dry it off for a few days, and then see what it is like. If the compost is useable, spread it around your flowers as a top dressing. If it is still a mess, tip it onto your conventional compost heap – don't waste it!

If it is the bottom tray that is bogged down, check the sump as if it has filled right up (after heavy rain, for instance), the bottom tray will have been flooded. Drain the sump and leave it for a few days. The bottom tray contains the waste that has been most highly composted and in all probability will probably dry out and be ready for use.

The problem has usually been caused by insufficient carbon-based material being added to the wormery. Remember - add waste; add paper; add waste; add cardboard. Brainwash yourself to follow this doctrine.

Finally, don't forget that some food simply smells! Cabbage and other greens smell pretty strong when they are rotting, and onions are also pungent.

84

When I open my wormery, swarms of tiny black midges fly out!

These are fruit flies and they will at some time appear in any system that isn't completely sealed. There are various other flies such as vinegar flies and mushroom flies that may be in the swarm, but they are all small and black and pretty hard to tell apart. To me they are all fruit flies. They are useful to the composting process as they lay their eggs in the waste and then the grubs hatch out and feed on it, their excreta adding to the bacterial mix. I tend to ignore them, but if your wormery is indoors you will soon get fed up with them invading every room. The only way to get rid of them is to cover the waste in your wormery with a layer of soil or shredded paper so that the adult flies cannot reach the waste to lay their eggs. Don't be tempted to use fly spray in your wormery!

My wormery looks to be in good condition, but all my worms are dead!

If the wormery has not been subject to intense cold, then the most likely culprit is chemical contamination. Have you added any animal manure from livestock that has been recently wormed? Has insecticide been used near the wormery? Had any fruit skins in the waste been sprayed? Adding salty food is another possibility.

The fluid in my sump smells absolutely foul, and there are several dead worms drowned in it!

Situation pretty much normal, I'm afraid. The sump is the main bad point with stacking systems. If your system doesn't have built-in worm escape ramps make sure you put some cobblestones or a brick in the bottom, and drain your sump and check the contents at least once a week.

I'm not entirely convinced that worms do actually manage to get out of the sump via ramps, but at least they can get above the water level and avoid drowning, and you can rescue them when you carry out your regular checks. The dreadful smell is due to the millions of anaerobic bacteria living in the rich stagnant water, plus, of course, the decomposing worms!

Yuk! My wormery is full of fleas!

A wormery is way too moist to have fleas living in it. You are no doubt referring to hundreds of tiny white creatures hopping all over the place when you open the lid. You should be pleased as these are springtails and they are great composters. They are harmless to both yourself and your worms, so don't worry about them – even if there seem to be thousands of them. When climate and food supply are perfect they can reproduce at a truly astonishing rate and appear to be taking the place over.

Yuk! My wormery is full of mould!

Great! Ring the dinner gong to call your worms to lunch. Worms don't really eat much of the kitchen waste itself that you put in your bin, but they do eat the bacteria, mould and other creatures that live on the food and help it to decompose. We really do want to see mould and fungi growing in the waste. Just take care that you don't add too much waste so that the worms can't cope with it all. If there are worms up on the surface feeding when you open the bin then it is time to add a bit more waste. If not then wait a while.

Yuk! My wormery is swarming with ants!

If they have built a nest then your wormery is definitely too dry – water the contents with a watering can every day for a week and disturb the ants by digging in their nest with a hand fork. This should persuade them that there are more desirable places to live. If there is a constant stream of ants coming and going, but no nest, then they have found something yummy and are carrying it back to their nest.

Standing the legs of the wormery in a container full of water will stop their thieving, but watch out for ants wearing tiny water wings swimming across your moat.

Yuk! I added worm compost to my pot plants and now my windowsill is covered in creepy crawlies!

Don't exaggerate! What did you expect? Worm compost is a living thing, full of microbes and the eggs of various creatures that live in it. If you happen to add any to your flower pot, the chances are that the creatures will stay in the pot and complete their life cycle and die. The exceptions are fruit flies and other small midges, which may well decide that the wide open spaces of your living room are worth checking out for decaying food, but there are only likely to be a few from such a small top-up of compost. If it worries you, heat the compost up first in your microwave before you next feed your plants; this will eradicate any pesky fly eggs.

It is very cold and my worms are dead!

If you were stranded on a mountainside in a blizzard with no warm clothing you would die too, so why are you puzzled that your worms die in the cold? Their home – the compost – freezes solid, and the poor worms (which have a very high water content) freeze solid too.

You may find that your wormery re-colonises itself in the spring when any cocoons hatch, or you may have to buy fresh worms. Either way, next winter move your wormery somewhere frost proof or insulate it against the cold.

I started my wormery off yesterday, and all my worms have escaped overnight!

It is unlikely that they have all escaped, but it is possible. Your new worms were unhappy with the nesting material as it was too different from the bedding that they were familiar with, and so they looked for somewhere more comfortable. This can happen with coir block bedding. Empty out you wormery and find a worm supplier who dispatches them in vermicompost bedding. Always try to include some of the old worm compost to give the worms a good start if you are re-starting a wormery or starting off an extra one,

I started off my tray wormery system yesterday and a LOT of worms are in the sump today!

Did you place some newspapers or a sheet of cardboard in the bottom

of the first tray? If not, the bedding and the worms can just sift through the mesh base and end up in the sump. You are lucky that there will be no fluid in the sump this early, so your worms will have survived their little trip. Empty the tray, cover the mesh with paper or cardboard, and then tip the nesting material and worms back in – you (and your worms!) have had a lucky escape!

My worms are all over the inside of the lid, and stuck to the sides – are they trying to escape?

In a word – yes. Check the compost to see if it is dry. If it is (which it almost certainly is) then they are trying to keep themselves hydrated using the condensation on the inner surfaces. Give the compost a gentle sprinkling from a watering can, preferably with rain water if possible.

If the bin contents are wet then the system is almost certainly turning anaerobic and you need to act fast! Take action as in "my wormery smells awful" above.

I have seen rats around my bin!

Have you put meat or fish in your wormery? If so it is your own fault as the smell will have attracted them! Rats (and mice) are opportunists who are always on the look-out for an easy meal. If you are using a plastic system you are reasonably safe from mice, but rats can gnaw their way in if they can smell something tasty. If you are using a large outdoor wormery such as the pallet DIY wormery then they have several ways in – under, over or through! If you haven't constructed it with the built-in defences as detailed in the section earlier in this book then your only options are a trap or poison. I regularly get rats attracted to my chickens on the allotments, and I use a humane rat/squirrel trap that catches them alive. Be warned that they scream at you, and it is a very unpleasant sound! You still have the problem of what to do with them as releasing them somewhere else isn't an option, as you are just passing the problem to somebody else. Shooting them is the most humane method of destroying them.

Poison is another method I resort to, using a bait box that prevents other animals getting at the contents. Extreme care has to be exercised to keep the poison away from children and domestic animals.

Curiously, I have found that slugs and snails love the rat poison that I use - I have no idea whether it actually works on them too, but I do hope so!

Mice, voles, moles and shrews can all invade a large bed system. Shrews and moles particularly love a tasty worm, and a wire netting base and solid cover are the only way to keep them out.

My worms must be breeding well as I have hundreds of tiny white baby worms in my bin!

Er, no you don't, you have potworms. Baby worms have a red line running through them when they are first born, and later they look just like mum and dad, or should that be mumdad as worms have both sexes? Potworms are another welcome visitor to your wormery as they help with composting. Their appearance in large numbers may, however, be an indication that the compost is veering towards becoming acidic, so add some shredded paper into the mix if you think this is likely. You don't want the bin to become overly acidic as this will lead to anaerobic bacteria taking over.

How often should I add the lime that was supplied with my wormery kit?

I have several bags of lime that were supplied with some of my wormeries and I haven't even opened any of them yet. I am more likely to spread the contents on my allotments where I intend to grow brassicas (cabbages and sprouts to the uninitiated) than use them in my wormeries. It is far better to keep your bin in a stable condition by mixing paper and cardboard with your waste than to try to alter the balance drastically with lime, as you have no idea what effect it will have upon the millions of microscopic creatures living there.

My wormery came with a bag of worm food. How often should I use it?

Rarely is the answer as simple as just a light sprinkling very occasionally. When it runs out don't bother buying any more. Spend your money on something useful instead, like buying another copy of this book for a friend! If you are adding a good mix of fruit and vegetable trimmings, stale bread, tea bags, plus of course paper and cardboard, nothing else is really necessary. If you really want to give your worms a treat, add some well rotted horse manure to their bin.

My worms have eaten the moisture mat that came with my wormery!

Of course they have, and it was very tasty too! Don't bother buying another one. A couple of sheets of damp shredded newspaper on top of the waste will do the job just as well, and the worms will eat that too.

My wife tipped the lawn clippings into the worm bin and now all the worms are dead!

Get a new wife. Grass cuttings heat up enormously as they start to decompose and your worms have been cooked. Never add fresh cuttings to your wormery. Small quantities of clippings that have already been dried and partially composted on your traditional compost heap are acceptable, as are weeds that have not seeded, but the emphasis is on the words "small quantities".

My worms died. Should I buy one of the wormery recovery kits that I have seen advertised?

Nope, because if you killed the last lot, you will probably kill the next lot too unless you alter your management methods. Worms don't just die without a reason and these kits are not a magical cure for mismanagement.

They usually consist of little more than some fresh coir bedding, a bag of lime, a bag of worm food and some fresh worms. Re-read this book, find a worm retailer that supplies them in worm compost bedding and start again.

Are worms edible?

Well, ask any two-year old and they will probably say yes!

The easy answer is that yes they are, because they are largely protein, and they have undoubtedly been some part of Aboriginal diets over the millennia.

I've seen plenty of worm recipes and preparation instructions and undoubtedly Hugh Fearnley-Whittingstall could come up with a gourmet worm dish fit for a king, but for me they are a big "no" I'm afraid. Whilst I have eaten road kill deer and thoroughly enjoyed it, I have never been hungry enough to pick on a poor earthworm.

Who knows though, they could be the answer to a global food shortage at some time in the future.

Finally, don't let any of the above horror stories scare you away from running a wormery. Having read and digested this book, you should be competent enough to run a wormery correctly, and so you will be unlikely to experience many of the problems that can occur.

Most of the wormeries that are sold these days are pretty easy to keep running in good condition with happy worms as long as you use common sense. By the time that you progress to some of the larger home-made designs you will have learned from any mistakes that you made along the way, and should be able to cope with anything that goes wrong.

And Finally.....

Well-produced worm compost is better for your plants than just about any other form of compost and beats shop-bought feeds and fertilisers hands down. You rarely see worm compost for sale in garden centres, and when you do it is more expensive than most chemical or other organic fertilisers. This is because it takes a long time to produce – only the worms can do it.

A large chemical plant with a mechanised production line can manufacture a sack of chemical fertiliser in seconds, and organic feeds are generally only a mix of ingredients and can be produced with similar speed. Worm compost is a living feed, still containing the millions of bacteria and moulds etc. that will enliven the soil around your plants and supply slow-release nutrients that are very difficult to produce synthetically. The compost will attract the worms living in the soil around your plants, and their activities will improve the drainage and aeration for your flowers, vegetables or fruit trees.

I have a vision that as word gradually spreads throughout the "grow your own" and farming communities, everybody will want to use worm compost, and I believe that eventually most homes will have a wormery in the garden.

Local councils will be running large wormery beds to process domestic and food industry waste. Years ago school canteens and other catering establishments emptied their slops into bins and the local piggery collected them to use the waste to feed their pigs. Swine fever put a stop to that and it is now illegal to feed kitchen waste to most livestock, but there is no reason why it shouldn't be fed to worms. Cider makers will be saving the apple pulp from their presses, and breweries will send the spent malt hops and yeast to the local municipal wormery where it will all be processed into worm compost. Councils will sell the compost to the gardening sector and earn millions of pounds, which will mean that instead of increasing our Council Tax to cover the cost of dealing with our domestic waste, they will be able to reduce our taxes by 10%.....

Yeah, okay, now I'm dreaming!

I do hope that this book has convinced you that worms aren't at all boring, and that it has inspired you to start a wormery.

Whilst for now we may be considered a bit "odd," future generations sitting in their eco-friendly houses heated by wave powered free electricity and driving cars whose batteries last for one thousand miles before needing a recharge, will look back and see us as pioneers for a greener lifestyle.

Useful Contacts and Addresses

Bubble House Worms
Chapel Lane
Bransford
Worcestershire
WR6 5JG
Tel: 01886 832559
Email: info@bubblehouseworms.
com
www.bubblehouseworms.com
Supplying wormeries, worms
in compost, bokashi and
vermicompost

Bucket of Worms
Ley Farm
Monkleigh
Bideford
North Devon
EX39 5JZ
Tel: 01237 473336
Email: enquiries@bucketofworms.
co.uk
www.bucketofworms.co.uk
Supplying wormeries and worms
in compost

Green Gardener
Brook Hill
Brundall Road
Blofield
Norfolk NR13 4LB
Tel: 01603 715096
Email: jon@greengardener.co.uk
www.greengardener.co.uk
Supplying wormeries, worms
and bokashi

Nurturing Nature
1 Banbury Drive
Great Sankey
Warrington
WA5 1HW
Tel: 01925 452819
Email: enquiries4nature@nurturing
nature.co.uk
www.nurturingnature.co.uk
Supplying Waste Buster wormeries

The Organic Gardening Catalogue
Riverdene Business Park
Molesey Road
Hersham
Surrey
KT12 4RG
Tel: 01932 252707
Email: contact form on website
www.organicgardeningcatalogue.
com
Supplying worms and wormeries

Original Organics
Unit 9 Langlands Business Park
Uffculme
Cullompton
Devon, EX15 3DA
Tel: 0800 1209676
Email: contact form on website
www.originalorganics.co.uk
Supplying wormeries and a range
of garden equipment

The Recycle Works
Unit 1 Bee Mil
Ribchester
Nr. Longridge
PR3 3XJ
Tel: 01254 820088
Email: Sylvia@recycleworks.co.uk
www.recycleworks.co.uk
Supplying Waste Buster wormeries
and worms

Vermisell Town & Country
Supplies
Sandy Gap Cottage
Burton in Kendal
Carnforth
Lancs. LA6 1NT
Tel: 01829 749276
Email: ino@vermisell.co.uk
www.vermisell.co.uk
Supplying wormeries, garden
supplies, bushes trees and plants

Wiggly Wigglers
Lower Blakemere Farm
Blakemere
Herefordshire
HR2 9PX
Tel: 0181 500391
Email: wiggly@wigglywigglers.
co.uk
www.wigglywigglers.co.uk
Supplying wormeries, wildlife food
and housing, books, veg seeds and
Bokashi

The Worm Hotel
Shrubbs Farm
Edgfield
Norfolk
NR24 2AT
Tel: 01263 587722
Email: Contact form on website
www.thewormhotel.com
Supplying worms and wormeries

Worm City Ltd.
128 Kingfisher Way
Ringwood
Hants.
BH24 3LN
Tel: 0800 141598
Email: Contact form on website
www.wormcity.co.uk
Supplying wormeries, Bokashi
equipment and supplies

Worms Direct
Drylands
Ulting
Nr. Maldon
Essex
CM9 6QS
Tel: 01245 381933
Email: enquiries@wormsdirect.
co.uk
www.wormsdirectuk.co.uk
Supplying wormeries, worms in
compost and consultancy

Glossary

Acidic – referring to pH levels that are measured below neutral, ie. measuring below level 7. Strongly acidic conditions are not desirable in a wormery.

Aerobic – requiring oxygen to live. Aerobic bacteria are what we want living in our wormeries.

Albumen – a protein rich fluid, as in the "white" of a chicken's egg. Albumen is secreted into the cocoons by worms to nourish the young.

Alkaline – the opposite end of the pH scale from acidic. Alkalinity is also not wanted in a wormery, although worms can tolerate mild alkalinity.

Anaerobic – referring to life that does not require oxygen to live. Anaerobic conditions are the enemy of all worm keepers.

Bedding – the material that you place in your wormery as an initial home for your worms, sometimes also called nesting material (although I have yet to see a worm's nest).

Bokashi – a system of composting kitchen waste in sealed bins using activated bran to break down the waste material.

Cast – worm cast or castings are the pure excreta of the worms. If you leave your wormery for long enough you will be left with pure worm cast.

Clitellum – sometimes called the saddle, the clitellum produces mucus which hardens to form cocoons. The clitellum (the swollen section just back from the head) only forms in worms that are mature and in breeding condition. The clitellum also produces another type of mucus that helps to stick worms together during mating.

Cocoon – the egg chamber "purse" produced by the worms in which fertilised eggs are stored while they develop.

Compost – totally decomposed organic material used as a planting medium or fertiliser. In our case we are looking to produce compost produced by worms and microbes.

Compost heap – a traditional composting method, piling up organic material in the open air and allowing it to rot down to produce compost.

Decomposing – rotting and breaking down into the basic elements. Bacteria decompose kitchen waste so that it can be eaten by our worms and broken down still further.

Ecosystem – a complete enclosed system of inter-reacting organisms.

Fertiliser – something added to soil to improve nutrient levels to promote plant growth. Worm castings prove a better fertiliser than most synthetically produced soil improvers.

Gizzard – a muscular sac through which food is passed and broken down, using a combination of muscle contractions and grit swallowed by the worm before passing through the digestive system.

Hermaphrodite – a life form that possesses both male and female sex organs, and in some cases does not require a mate in order to reproduce.

Hibernation – a dormant state when a creature's metabolism slows right down and it moves and eats very little, usually during cold weather.

Humus – the minute organic residue

in the top layer of soil, essential to moisture retention.

Invertebrates – creatures with no backbone like worms.

Kitchen waste – the name given to the food that we give to our worms consisting of fruit and vegetable clippings, tea bags, egg shells, stale bread etc.

Leaching, leachate – the washing out of nutrients or chemicals and the rich liquid that results from this process.

Leaf mould – fallen leaves that have decomposed, producing a rich dark soil-like material. Leaf mould makes a good worm nesting material or can be mixed with worm compost to produce a very effective fertiliser.

Lime – calcium carbonate, a sedimentary rock reduced to a powder and supplied with some wormeries to reduce acidity. Not recommended for use by the author as it will change pH levels too quickly and may harm the friendly microbes in your wormery.

Microbes – tiny creatures that live in wormeries, but cannot be seen with the naked eye.

Mucus – a slimy coating produced by worms to smooth their passage through the soil and to help them to retain their water content. Mucus produced by the clitellum hardens to form a cocoon.

Mulch – a top-coating of worm cast, leaf mould or compost applied to the surface of the soil around a plant or shrub to serve as a fertiliser, moisture-retainer, weed suppressant – or all three.

Nematode – a parasitic worm that lives inside a host and feeds from it, often causing the death of the host.

Nematodes can be used to control slugs, aphids and other pests.

pH – the pH scale (potential hydrogen) is used to identify whether (in our case) soil is alkaline or acidic on a scale of 1 to 14. A worm is most comfortable in slightly acidic soil (5 or 6) but can cope with a wide range of soil types.

Parasite – an organism which lives on or within another organism and draws its sustenance from its host. This may be a creature (for instance a flea) or a plant (mistletoe).

Pathogen – a living organism which may cause disease.

Pheromone – a chemical created by an organism which is designed to create a reaction in another creature of the same species.

Setae – the minute bristles along a worm's body that help it to move.

Vermicast – consisting of pure worm castings, virtually all organic material having been decomposed or digested.

Vermicompost – a mixture of worm castings and the remnants of various organic materials, microbes, worms and their cocoons.

Vermiculture – the breeding of earthworms.

Worm bin – anything used as a home for a colony of worms. Early wormeries were modified dustbins and the name is now universally used for any worm farming container, regardless of size.

The Good Life Press Ltd.
The Old Pigsties
Clifton Fields
Lytham Road
Preston PR4 0XG
01772 633444

The Good Life Press Ltd. publishes a wide range of titles for the smallholder, 'goodlifer' and farmer. We also publish **Home Farmer,** the monthly magazine for anyone who wants to grab a slice of the good life - whether they live in the country or the city. Other titles of interest include:

A Guide to Traditional Pig Keeping by Carol Harris
An Introduction to Keeping Cattle by Peter King
An Introduction to Keeping Sheep by J. Upton/D. Soden
Any Fool Can Be a Middle Aged Downshifter by Mike Woolnough
Build It! by Joe Jacobs
Build It!....With Pallets by Joe Jacobs
Craft Cider Making by Andrew Lea
Flowerpot Farming by Jayne Neville
Grow and Cook by Brian Tucker
How to Butcher Livestock and Game by Paul Peacock
Making Country Wines, Ales and Cordials by Brian Tucker
Making Jams and Preserves by Diana Sutton
No Time To Grow? by Tim Wootton
Precycle! by Paul Peacock
Raising Chickens for Eggs and Meat by Mike Woolnough
Raising Goats - Meat-Dairy-Fibre by Felicity Stockwell
Showing Sheep by Sue Kendrick
The Bread and Butter Book by Diana Sutton
The Cheese Making Book by Paul Peacock
The Frugal Life by Piper Terrett
The Pocket Guide to Wild Food by Paul Peacock
The Polytunnel Companion by Jayne Neville
The Sausage Book by Paul Peacock
The Sheep Book for Smallholders by Tim Tyne
The Smallholders Guide to Animal Ailments edited by Russell Lyon BVM&S MRCVS
The Smoking and Curing Book by Paul Peacock
The Urban Farmer's Handbook by Paul Peacock

www.goodlifepress.co.uk
www.homefarmer.co.uk